Chelsea vs. Arsenal
The First 150 Derby Games

BEST WISHES

Gary Smith, MAY 2004

Chelsea vs. Arsenal
The First 150 Derby Games

by

Gary Watton

Paperback ISBN 1 903970 68 7

**Published
by**

Central Publishing Limited
Royd Street Offices
Milnsbridge
Huddersfield
West Yorkshire
HD3 4QY

www.centralpublishing.co.uk

Introduction

Arsenal and Chelsea have a history – together. Their duel is the longest running London Derby – at least so far as they were the first two football clubs from the capital to compete in the old First Division. Ever since the Edwardian age, North and West London's finest have continued to engage in their local skirmish on a regular basis – normally twice a year. Although this book confirms every Chelsea fan's worst fears that Arsenal more often than not held the upper hand, there are enough glorious moments as well as setbacks for both sets of supporters to focus on.

With the Chelsea – Arsenal clash on Sunday September 1st 2002 representing the 150th major contest (excluding friendly games) between the two London rivals, this publication is a 'celebration' of the first 150 derby matches. Rather than dwell on a plethora of details in each encounter, the author has chosen only to record the bare facts, concentrating instead upon the impact that each result had on the development or otherwise of each football club. Therefore, this work aims to survey the peaks and troughs that Arsenal and Chelsea have both experienced over the last century against the backdrop of their derby fixtures.

Arsenal and Chelsea draw larger home crowds than any other London clubs; and for the last half a dozen years they have produced London's top two teams. In all probability, this state of affairs will continue into the near future. Therefore, to say that this derby has once again assumed increasing importance is an understatement. Incidentally, one has only to take a glance at the crowd figures for some of the contests in the 1930s in order to gain some idea of just how important an attraction this derby was (and still is) for many people.

Arsenal vs Chelsea
The First 150 Derby Games

CHELSEA 2 WOOLWICH ARSENAL 1; November 9th 1907 (Crowd 55,000) Scorers:(Home team first) Hilsdon (2); C. Satterthwaite.

The Blues and the Gunners first locked horns together in Edwardian times when Sir Henry Campbell-Bannerman was the Liberal Prime Minister. Newly-promoted Chelsea were enjoying their first ever season in Division One and they took full honours courtesy of a double from England international centre-forward George 'Gatling Gun' Hilsdon. Charlie Satterthwaite, one of two brothers who played for Woolwich Arsenal was on target for the away team but his goal could not prevent a narrow defeat. David Calderhead's team were competing in their first London derby in the top flight and the huge attendance set the tone for the subsequent contests which continued to draw large crowds. Indeed, the largest home crowd of the season witnessed this clash at Stamford Bridge.

CHELSEA	WOOLWICH ARSENAL
1 Whiting	1 Ashcroft
2 Cameron	2 Gray
3 Miller	3 Sharp
4 Key	4 Dick
5 Stark	5 Sands
6 Birnie	6 McEachrane
7 Moran	7 Garbutt
8 Rouse	8 Coleman

9 Hilsdon	9 Kyle
10 Windridge	10 Satterthwaite
11 Fairgray	11 Neave

WOOLWICH ARSENAL 0 CHELSEA 0; March 7th 1908 (Crowd: 30,000)

The second ever London derby in the First Division ended in stalemate. No score draws have been few and far between in contests between Arsenal and Chelsea, but this was one of the few occasions when either side failed to 'trouble the scorer.' The west Londoners could draw satisfaction from a season end position of thirteenth which enabled them to finish narrowly ahead of their London rivals. The Gunners took the opportunity many times to avenge this state of affairs.

WOOLWICH ARSENAL	CHELSEA
1 Ashcroft	1 Whitley
2 Gray	2 Cameron
3 Sharp	3 Miller
4 Ducat	4 McRoberts
5 Sands	5 Stark
6 McEachrane	6 Birnie
7 Lee	7 Brawn
8 Lewis	8 Humphreys
9 Freeman	9 Hilsdon
10 Satterthwaite	10 Windridge
11 Neave	11 Fairgray

SEASON 1907-8:
CHELSEA:

Finished 13th; Won 14; Drew 8; Lost 16; Goals for 53; Against 62; Points 36
WOOLWICH ARSENAL:
Finished 14th; Won 12; Drew 12; Lost 14; Goals for 51; Against 63; Points 36

CHELSEA 1 WOOLWICH ARSENAL 2; November 28th 1908 (Crowd 55,000) Scorers: Hilsdon; Greenaway Lewis

George Hilsdon found the back of the net against Woolwich Arsenal again but could not stop the away team recording their first win over the Blues. Goals from David Greenaway and Charlie Lewis ensured that the south Londoners claimed both points. For the second successive year Stamford Bridge's biggest crowd of the season appears at the capital's only London derby from Division One.

CHELSEA	WOOLWICH ARSENAL
1 Whitley	1 McDonald
2 Cameron	2 Shaw
3 Miller	3 Gray
4 Warren	4 Ducat
5 McRoberts	5 Sands
6 Birnie	6 McEachrane
7 Brawn	7 Greenaway
8 Rouse	8 Lewis
9 Hilsdon	9 Raybould
10 Windridge	10 Fitchie
11 Fairgray	11 Satterthwaite

WOOLWICH ARSENAL 0 CHELSEA 0; April 3rd 1909 (Crowd: 20,000)

History repeated itself when the Pensioners came to the Manor Ground and earned a share of the spoils as both the hosts and guests failed to find the target. One major consolation for the home team was their loftier league position at the end of the season. Indeed, both clubs achieved their highest finishes yet in the Football League. Their supremacy in London would find a new challenge in the following season when newly-promoted Tottenham Hotspur would be joining them.

WOOLWICH ARSENAL	CHELSEA
1 McDonald	1 Whitley
2 Shaw	2 Cartwright
3 Gray	3 Walton
4 Ducat	4 Humphreys
5 Sands	5 Birnie
6 McEachrane	6 Freeman
7 Greenaway	7 Brawn
8 Raybould	8 Reilly
9 Beney	9 Hilsdon
10 Fitchie	10 Windridge
11 Neave	11 Douglas

SEASON 1908-9
WOOLWICH ARSENAL:
Finished 6th; Won 14; Drew 10; Lost 14; Goals for 52; Against 49; Points 38
CHELSEA:

Finished 11th; Won 14; Drew 9; Lost 15; Goals for 56; Against 61; Points 37

WOOLWICH ARSENAL 3 CHELSEA 2; September 25th 1909 (Crowd 20,000) Scorers: Lee (2) Greenaway; Wileman Fairgray

A double from Harold Lee as well as a goal from David Greenaway provided the Gunners with their first home win against the Pensioners at the third time of asking. Norrie Fairgray and Arthur Wileman both scored for the visitors, but their efforts were to be in vain. Even more tragic for Wileman was that he was one of the many young footballers who gave service to their country during the 'Great War' and he lost his life when he was killed in action at Ypres in March 1918.

WOOLWICH ARSENAL	CHELSEA
1 McDonald	1 Whitley
2 Gray	2 Walton
3 Cross	3 Cameron
4 Dick	4 Warren
5 Sands	5 Ormiston
6 McEachrane	6 Birnie
7 Greenaway	7 Brawn
8 Lewis	8 Wileman
9 Lee	9 Jones
10 Satterthwaite	10 Windridge
11 Neave	11 Fairgray

CHELSEA 0 WOOLWICH ARSENAL 1; March 28th 1910 (Crowd 40,000) Scorer: McGibbon

George Morell's team completed the first double in contests between the Arsenal and Chelsea courtesy of a goal from Charles McGibbon. Of more significance was the fact that this result effectively rescued the men in red from a dreaded prospect of relegation whilst condemning the home side to such a fate. However, the Gunners had little to smile about in a season that saw them eclipsed by neighbours Tottenham Hotspur as London's premier team. McGibbon incidentally was playing in his debut and was a non-commissioned army officer at the time.

CHELSEA	WOOLWICH ARSENAL
1 Whitley	1 H. McDonald
2 Bettridge	2 D. McDonald
3 Cameron	3 Shaw
4 Taylor	4 Ducat
5 Ormiston	5 Thomson
6 Downing	6 McKinnon
7 Douglas	7 Buckenham
8 Wileman	8 Lewis
9 Jones	9 McGibbon
10 Freeman	10 Lawrence
11 Holden	11 Heppinstall

SEASON 1909-10:

WOOLWICH ARSENAL:
Finished 18th; Won 11; Drew 9; Lost 18; Goals for 37; Against 67; Points 31
CHELSEA:
Finished 19th; Won 11; Drew 7; Lost 20; Goals for 47; Against 70; Points 29

WOOLWICH ARSENAL 0 CHELSEA 1; October 12th 1912 (Crowd 22,000) Scorer: Bridgeman

After a two-year exile in the Second Division the team from west London were back with a vengeance when they sank the south Londoners by the narrowest of margins. William Bridgeman was responsible for the goal which earned Chelsea their first-ever away win in the derby fixture at the fourth attempt. This was the last time that the Arsenal hosted this match at the Manor Ground. Future battles between the two London giants would take place at Highbury – north of the River Thames – as well as at Stamford Bridge.

WOOLWICH ARSENAL	CHELSEA
1 Crawford	1 Brebner
2 Shaw	2 Bettridge
3 Peart	3 Cameron
4 Thomas	4 Taylor
5 Sands	5 Ormiston
6 McKinnon	6 Downing
7 Greenaway	7 Douglas
8 Common	8 Whittingham
9 Mclaughlan	9 Woodward
10 Randall	10 Dodd
11 Winship	11 Bridgeman

CHELSEA 1 WOOLWICH ARSENAL 1; February 15th 1913 (Crowd 20,000) Scorers: Ford; Burrell

Although a George Burrell goal provided the visitors with a share of the points, this satisfactory result could not prevent the away team from sliding toward their only relegation from the First Division. Woolwich Arsenal went on to score fewer goals than anyone else in the league and also to concede more goals than all other teams. Harry Ford helped the Blues to a point with his goal but Chelsea had little to cheer about, finishing perilously close to the drop zone. Worse still, Tottenham Hotspur ended the season as London's top team!

CHELSEA	WOOLWICH ARSENAL
1 Molyneux	1 McDonald
2 Bettridge	2 Shaw
3 Sharp	3 Fidler
4 Taylor	4 Grant
5 Calderhead	5 Sands
6 Harwood	6 Graham
7 Ford	7 Greenaway
8 Brown	8 Lewis
9 Turnbull	9 Stonley
10 Woodward	10 Devine
11 Bridgeman	11 Burrell

SEASON 1913-13:
CHELSEA:
Finished 18th; Won 11; Drew 6; Lost 21; Goals for 51; Against 73; Points 28
WOOLWICH ARSENAL:
Finished 20th; Won 3; Drew 12; Lost 23; Goals for 26; Against 74; Points 18

CHELSEA 1 WOOLWICH ARSENAL 0; January 30th 1915 (Crowd 40,372) FA Cup 2nd round; Scorer: Halse

The Pensioners emerged victorious from the first cup encounter between Arsenal and Chelsea courtesy of a goal from England international Harold Halse. Halse had already collected a FA Cup winner's medal with Manchester United and Aston Villa, and in this year he added a loser's medal to his tally. The Arsenal were a Second Division outfit at this time and were probably glad that the interruption of total war enabled them to re-group and come back stronger in the inter-war years. They would be presented with ample opportunities in future years to avenge this cup defeat by the Blues.

CHELSEA	WOOLWICH ARSENAL
1 Molyneux	1 Lievesley
2 Bettridge	2 Shaw
3 Harrow	3 Benson
4 Taylor	4 Grant
5 Logan	5 Buckley
6 Abrams	6 McKinnon
7 Ford	7 Rutherford
8 Halse	8 Flanagan
9 Thomson	9 King
10 Croal	10 Bradshaw
11 McNeil	11 Lewis

ARSENAL 1 CHELSEA 1; December 6th 1919 (Crowd 50,000) Scorers: White; Cock

Both Arsenal and Chelsea were recipients of extreme good fortune when the English football league was re-structured after the cessation of hostilities. In Chelsea's case they had finished nineteenth in the last league season which ended in the spring of 1915 and might normally have expected to be relegated, but in the abnormal circumstances of a world war the Blues received a reprieve which allowed them bizarrely to take their place in the top flight once again. The Gunners meanwhile secured the most outrageous of promotions when they were catapulted back into the elite after having finished 'only' fifth in the Second Division back in 1915. Neither Barnsley nor Wolverhampton Wanderers who both finished ahead of Arsenal were permitted to join them in the First Division. For both Arsenal and Chelsea, the icing on their lucky cake was the relegation of Tottenham Hotspur to Division Two. The 'Spurs' evidently merited less sympathy from the powers that be.

Anyhow, in the first post-war tussle London's top two shared the points with Henry White scoring for the hosts and Jack Cock finding the target for the visitors; with the return to normality, it was business as usual in terms of the crowd size – a fairly big one to be precise.

ARSENAL	CHELSEA
1 Williamson	1 Hampton
2 Shaw	2 Bettridge
3 Bradshaw	3 Harrow
4 Butler	4 Middelboe
5 Sands	5 Ormiston
6 McKinnon	6 Dickie
7 Rutherford	7 Dale
8 White	8 Halse

9 Pagnam	9 Cock
10 Hardinge	10 Croal
11 Toner	11 McNeil

CHELSEA 3 ARSENAL 1; December 13th 1919 (Crowd 60,000) Scorers: Ford Cock McNeil; White

One week later and an even larger turnout of spectators greeted an impressive triumph for the home team. Not only were the Pensioners carrying on where they left off after enjoying war-time supremacy against the north Londoners, but they were in the midst of their best-ever football season. A journey as far as the semi-finals of the FA Cup as well as an encouraging top three finish in Division One appeared to indicate better times ahead. Henry White scored Arsenal's goal for the second successive week but his efforts were overshadowed by those of Jack Cock; Harry Ford and Robert McNeil who each ensured maximum points for David Calderhead's team.

CHELSEA	ARSENAL
1 Hampton	1 Williamson
2 Bettridge	2 Shaw
3 Harrow	3 Bradshaw
4 Middelboe	4 Butler
5 Wilding	5 Buckley
6 Logan	6 McKinnon
7 Ford	7 Rutherford
8 Halse	8 White
9 Cock	9 Pagnam
10 Croal	10 Hardinge
11 McNeil	11 Toner

SEASON 1919-20:
CHELSEA:
Finished 3rd; Won 22; Drew 5; Lost 15; Goals for 56;
Against 51; Points 49
ARSENAL:
Finished 10th; Won 15; Drew 12; Lost 15; Goals for 56;
Against 58; Points 42

CHELSEA 1 ARSENAL 2; December 4th 1920 (Crowd
60,000) Scorers: Cock; Pagnam (2)

For the second successive year the visit of London rivals
Arsenal drew Chelsea's second largest league crowd at
Stamford Bridge. On this occasion a Fred Pagnam double
ensured that the visitors would have fonder memories of
this contest. Jack Cock scored for the third consecutive
time against the Gunners but to no avail. At least the
Pensioners had the opportunity to redeem themselves the
following week when the return fixture would be played
out. This was the second of four back-to-back contests in
the years following the end of the Great War when the
Football League arranged matches in such a way that two
teams would enter into combat home and away against
each other in successive weeks, instead of the normal
practice of playing one another in two matches spread
over different parts of the season.

CHELSEA	ARSENAL
1 Hampton	1 Williamson
2 Bettridge	2 Shaw
3 Harrow	3 Hutchins

4 Middelboe	4 Baker
5 Wilding	5 Graham
6 Ward	6 McKinnon
7 Ford	7 Rutherford
8 Ferris	8 White
9 Cock	9 Pagnam
10 Croal	10 Blyth
11 McNeil	11 Paterson

ARSENAL 1 CHELSEA 1; December 11th 1920 (Crowd 50,000) Scorers: Blyth; Ferris

Ulsterman James Ferris scored for the visitors but his effort was not enough to achieve revenge for the previous week's setback thanks to a goal from Billy Blyth which ensured that Arsenal would share the spoils. The west Londoners' position as London's top team quickly came to a halt as a depressing slide into mediocrity began. Arsenal meanwhile maintained mid-table 'respectability' which in turn was spoiled by upstarts Tottenham Hotspur who overtook them in the London pecking order and went on to win their second FA Cup trophy.

ARSENAL	CHELSEA
1 Williamson	1 Hampton
2 Shaw	2 Bettridge
3 Hutchins	3 Harrow
4 Baker	4 Middelboe
5 Graham	5 Wilding
6 McKinnon	6 Ward
7 Rutherford	7 Ford
8 White	8 Ferris

9 Pagnam	9 Cock
10 Blyth	10 Croal
11 Paterson	11 McNeil

SEASON 1920-21:

ARSENAL:

Finished 9th; Won 15; Drew 14; Lost 13; Goals for 59; Against 63; Points 44

CHELSEA:

Finished 18th; Won 13; Drew 13; Lost 16; Goals for 48; Against 58; Points 39

CHELSEA 0 ARSENAL 2; December 31st 1921 (Crowd 50,000) Scorers: White Boreham

Henry White and Reg Boreham provided the goals which sealed a miserable end to the year for the Blues. The Gunners themselves were struggling to make much impression in the league and this victory would have given Arsenal much-needed relief from an unsatisfactory league campaign. Both clubs would have been hoping for better things in 1922, especially when they cast an envious eye in the direction of the fast improving Tottenham Hotspur.

CHELSEA	ARSENAL
1 Howard Baker	1 Williamson
2 Harrow	2 Bradshaw
3 Barrett	3 Hutchins
4 McKenzie	4 Milne
5 Wilding	5 Graham
6 Smith	6 Whittaker
7 Bell	7 Rutherford
8 Ford	8 Blyth

9 Cock
10 Croal
11 McNeil

9 White
10 Boreham
11 Toner

ARSENAL 1 CHELSEA 0; January 14th 1922 (Crowd 40,000) Scorer: Boreham

Reg Boreham scored again to complete Arsenal's second league double over the Pensioners. In spite of successive wins against their London rivals the Gunners found themselves in an uncomfortably low position at the end of the league season. The Blues meanwhile were already reeling from an early exit from the FA Cup, yet they managed to turn their season around when they embarked on a thirteen game unbeaten run which included a remarkable sequence of seven straight wins. A position of second however left Tottenham Hotspur as London's top performing team.

ARSENAL
1 Williamson
2 Bradshaw
3 Hutchins
4 Baker
5 Graham
6 Whittaker
7 Creegan
8 Blyth
9 White
10 Boreham
11 Toner

CHELSEA
1 Howard Baker
2 Harrow
3 Smith
4 McKenzie
5 Wilding
6 Middelboe
7 Bell
8 Ford
9 Hoddinott
10 Croal
11 McNeil

SEASON 1921-22:
CHELSEA:
Finished 9th; Won 17; Drew 12; Lost 13; Goals for 40; Against 43; Points 46
ARSENAL:
Finished 17th; Won 15; Drew 7; Lost 20; Goals for 47; Against 56; Points 37

CHELSEA 0 ARSENAL 0; February 17th 1923 (Crowd 45,000)

The Blues and Reds fought out a scoreless draw which only served to reinforce their mediocre under-achievers status in England's top league. With the advent of West Ham United imminent in the top flight, Arsenal and Chelsea were in danger of slipping further down London's pecking order.

CHELSEA	ARSENAL
1 Hampton	1 Robson
2 Smith	2 Mackie
3 Harrow	3 Kennedy
4 Priestley	4 Milne
5 Frew	5 Butler
6 Meehan	6 John
7 Linfoot	7 Rutherford
8 Ford	8 Blyth
9 Armstrong	9 Turnbull
10 Sharp	10 Baker
11 McNeil	11 Paterson

ARSENAL 3 CHELSEA 1; February 24th 1923 (Crowd 40,000) Scorers: Blyth (2) Baker; Ford

Harry Ford recorded his third goal against the Gunners – a full ten years after his first one. Nevertheless, his achievement was well and truly overshadowed by a double from Billy Blyth and a goal from Alf Baker which stretched Arsenal's unbeaten run against the Pensioners to six matches. The north Londoners finished the season in their now-familiar mid-table territory while the west London outfit flirted dangerously again with relegation.

ARSENAL	CHELSEA
1 Robson	1 Hampton
2 Mackie	2 Smith
3 Kennedy	3 Harrow
4 Milne	4 Priestley
5 Butler	5 Frew
6 John	6 Meehan
7 Rutherford	7 Linfoot
8 Blyth	8 Ford
9 Turnbull	9 Armstrong
10 Baker	10 Sharp
11 Paterson	11 McNeil

SEASON 1922-23:
ARSENAL:
Finished 11th; Won 16; Drew 10; Lost 16; Goals for 61; Against 62; Points 42
CHELSEA:
Finished 19th; Won 9; Drew 18; Lost 15; Goals for 45; Against 53; Points 36

ARSENAL 1 CHELSEA 0; December 29th 1923 (Crowd 38,000) Scorer: Turnbull

Bob Turnbull provided the only goal of this contest against a club which he would play for a few years later. In the meantime Turnbull went on to be Arsenal's leading scorer in a desperately disappointing season for them. The losers however were in even worse shape as relegation beckoned for them in 1924.

ARSENAL	CHELSEA
1 Robson	1 Marsh
2 Mackie	2 Smith
3 Baker	3 Harrow
4 Milne	4 Priestley
5 Graham	5 Wilding
6 Young	6 Meehan
7 Paterson	7 Castle
8 Blyth	8 Crawford
9 Turnbull	9 Wilson
10 Woods	10 Haywood
11 Haden	11 Ferguson

CHELSEA 0 ARSENAL 0; January 5th 1924 (Crowd 38,000)

For the fifth time in their last six matches, the Blues failed to score against their London rivals. Not even a run of four successive wins at the end of the league season could spare the Pensioners from the dreaded drop to the Second Division. Arsenal meanwhile finished a mere one point above the relegation zone. To make matters even worse, both Tottenham Hotspur and West Ham United ended the season in a higher position than both Arsenal and Chelsea. Six years would pass before the rivalry would be renewed by which time Arsenal would be transformed – courtesy of a certain Mr Herbert Chapman.

CHELSEA	ARSENAL
1 Marsh	1 Robson
2 Smith	2 Mackie
3 Harrow	3 Baker
4 Priestley	4 Milne
5 Wilding	5 Graham
6 Meehan	6 Voysey
7 Linfoot	7 Paterson
8 Bennett	8 Blyth
9 Wilson	9 Turnbull
10 Ferguson	10 Woods
11 McNeil	11 Haden

SEASON 1923-24:

ARSENAL:
Finished 19th; Won 12; Drew 9; Lost 21; Goals for 40; Against 63; Points 33
CHELSEA:
Finished 21st; Won 9; Drew 14; Lost 19; Goals for 31; Against 53; Points 32

ARSENAL 2 CHELSEA 0; January 11th 1930 (Crowd 55,579) FA Cup 4th Round; Scorers: Lambert Bastin

The north Londoners asserted their superiority over their Second Division opponents courtesy of goals from Jack Lambert and the prolific Cliff Bastin. This triumph launched a prolonged challenge for the FA Cup which took the Gunners all the way to their second final where they made amends for their narrow defeat in 1927.

Jack Lambert was among the goals in the final when Arsenal finished their Cup campaign as they started it with a 2-0 victory. Alf Baker, Joe Hulme, David Jack and Tom Parker all shared the distinction of playing in Arsenal's first two finals. In spite of this defeat, it was not all doom and gloom for the Blues because an impressive run of form after this contest enabled them to escape out of the Second Division and re-join the elite where they would have the opportunity to re-acquaint themselves on a more regular basis with the formidable Gunners.

ARSENAL
1 Lewis
2 Parker
3 Hapgood
4 Haynes
5 Roberts
6 John
7 Hulme
8 Jack
9 Lambert
10 Thompson
11 Bastin

CHELSEA
1 Millington
2 Smith
3 Law
4 Russell
5 Rodger
6 Bishop
7 Crawford
8 Wilson
9 Mills
10 Miller
11 Pearson

CHELSEA 1 ARSENAL 5; November 29th 1930 (Crowd 74,667) Scorers: Law (Pen); Jack (3) Lambert Williams

The largest yet recorded attendance figure greeted the resumption of Arsenal and Chelsea's local feud in the First Division. The crowd was treated to an awesome show of finishing from the visitors. Despite a penalty from Scottish international full-back Tommy Law, the Pensioners had no answer to the Gunners' forays into the Blues' half of the field. Jack Lambert and Joey Williams both found the target but their own efforts were overshadowed by the heroics of England international David Jack who registered the first hat-trick in derby matches between the two combatants. Jack had made a name for himself by scoring in two victorious FA Cup finals for Bolton Wanderers, and his achievement in this match stands comparison with those previous glory days.

CHELSEA	ARSENAL
1 Millington	1 Harper
2 Odell	2 Parker
3 Law	3 Hapgood
4 Ferguson	4 Seddon
5 Rodger	5 Roberts
6 Bishop	6 John
7 Jackson	7 Williams
8 Cheyne	8 Jack
9 Pearson	9 Lambert
10 Wilson	10 James
11 Crawford	11 Bastin

CHELSEA 2 ARSENAL 1; January 24th 1931 (Crowd 62,475) FA Cup 4th Round; Scorers: Bishop Mills; Bastin

Only twelve months after their previous cup encounter the two London giants were drawn together again. The home supporters must have had a sense of foreboding after Arsenal had given their hosts a good spanking only eight weeks earlier. However, against all expectations, the Blues emerged triumphant thanks to goals from England international Sid Bishop and centre-forward George Mills. Cliff Bastin added to his FA Cup goal that he had scored against Chelsea a year earlier, but it was not enough to prevent something of a Cup shock. Arsenal were after all the reigning FA Cup holders but they merely re-doubled their efforts to pursue glory on another front – the league. The Pensioners meanwhile failed to match this performance when they were confronted with the apparently less formidable challenge of Birmingham City in the Sixth Round. The Blues had clearly treated this game as being their Cup Final. It was almost as if victory against other teams in the FA Cup was not of the same significance.

CHELSEA	ARSENAL
1 Millington	1 Harper
2 Barber	2 Parker
3 Law	3 Hapgood
4 Irving	4 Seddon
5 Townrow	5 Roberts
6 Bishop	6 John
7 Jackson	7 Hulme
8 Cheyne	8 Jack
9 Mills	9 Lambert
10 Wilson	10 James
11 Crawford	11 Bastin

ARSENAL 2 CHELSEA 1; April 4th 1931 (Crowd 53, 867) Scorers: Hulme Bastin; Gallacher

Cliff Bastin maintained his lethal scoring touch as the north Londoners moved another significant step towards their first Division One league championship. Joe Hulme provided the other goal for Herbert Chapman's team while Chelsea had to console themselves with a goal from pint-sized Scottish centre-forward Hugh Gallacher. The Blues had to be satisfied with a mid-table league position as they looked on with envied admiration at Arsenal's emphatic league triumph. Furthermore, the Gunners had stretched their unbeaten league run against Chelsea to ten matches.

ARSENAL	CHELSEA
1 Harper	1 Millington
2 Parker	2 Odell
3 Hapgood	3 Law
4 Jones	4 Irving
5 Roberts	5 Townrow
6 John	6 Bishop
7 Hulme	7 Pearson
8 Jack	8 Rankin
9 Lambert	9 Gallacher
10 James	10 Wilson
11 Bastin	11 Crawford

SEASON 1930-31:
ARSENAL:
Finished 1st; Won 28; Drew 10; Lost 4; Goals for 127; Against 59; Points 66
CHELSEA:

Finished 12th; Won 15; Drew 10; Lost 17; Goals for 64; Against 67; Points 40

CHELSEA 2 ARSENAL 1; November 21st 1931 (Crowd 64,427) Scorers: Rankin Gallacher; Lambert

The reigning league champions were humbled on this day as the Blues achieved their first league win against Arsenal for twelve years. Chief destroyers were the goal scorers John Rankin and Hughie Gallacher – both from Scotland. Jack Lambert recorded his third goal against Chelsea but the home team nevertheless held on for a narrow win which had stopped the rot. Arsenal at least remained firmly in contention for a possible second league Championship title.

CHELSEA	ARSENAL
1 Millington	1 Moss
2 Barber	2 Parker
3 Law	3 Hapgood
4 Carter	4 Jones
5 O'Dowd	5 Seddon
6 Bishop	6 John
7 Jackson	7 Hulme
8 Rankin	8 Jack
9 Gallacher	9 Lambert
10 Mills	10 James
11 Crawford	11 Bastin

ARSENAL 1 CHELSEA 1; April 2nd 1932 (Crowd 56,124) Scorers: Bastin; Gallacher

Goal scoring heroes Cliff 'Boy' Bastin and Hugh Gallacher ensured that the spoils would be shared as the two teams contrived to produce their first drawn encounter since 1924. The Blues had to content themselves with another mid-table position but could at least point to a journey to the semi-finals of the FA Cup as signs of progress. Best of all, they finished unbeaten against Arsenal and the three points that the Gunners dropped against Chelsea during the season made all the difference in determining that the north Londoners would narrowly fail to hold on to their league trophy. Furthermore, Arsenal had to settle for the role as bridesmaids in the FA Cup when they succumbed in the final to Chelsea's conquerors – the Magpies of Newcastle United.

ARSENAL	CHELSEA
1 Moss	1 Millington
2 Parker	2 Barber
3 Hapgood	3 Law
4 Jones	4 Russell
5 Roberts	5 O'Dowd
6 Male	6 Bishop
7 Hulme	7 Jackson
8 Jack	8 Cheyne
9 Lambert	9 Gallacher
10 John	10 Miller
11 Bastin	11 Pearson

SEASON 1931-2:
ARSENAL:
Finished 2nd; Won 22; Drew 10; Lost 10; Goals for 90; Against 48; Points 54

CHELSEA:
Finished 12th; Won 16; Drew 8; Lost 18; Goals for 69; Against 73; Points 40

ARSENAL 4 CHELSEA 1; December 10th 1932 (Crowd 53,206) Scores: Bastin (2) Coleman Hulme; Russell

Free-scoring Arsenal were making a determined bid to recapture the league championship and hapless Chelsea had no answer except for a rare goal from Scotsman William Russell. Cliff Bastin netted twice en route to a career total of 150 goals while Tim Coleman and Joe Hulme both weighed in with goals of their own. Having failed to overcome the Blues in the previous season, normal business was resumed by the mighty Arsenal.

ARSENAL	CHELSEA
1 Moss	1 Woodley
2 Male	2 Barber
3 Hapgood	3 Law
4 Hill	4 Russell
5 Roberts	5 O'Dowd
6 John	6 Rankin
7 Hulme	7 Crawford
8 Jack	8 Ferguson
9 Coleman	9 Gallacher
10 James	10 Miller
11 Bastin	11 Prout

CHELSEA 1 ARSENAL 3; April 22nd 1933 (Crowd 72,260) Scorers: Gallacher; Bastin (2) Jack

Another mammoth crowd was at Stamford Bridge to witness the Gunners complete another league double against the Blues. The last time that they achieved this feat in 1931 they went on to lift the league trophy. History repeated itself as Arsenal sealed their second championship title. Hughie Gallacher attempted to stem the tide by finding the net once again but deadly marksman Cliff Bastin recorded a double for the second time in the season against Chelsea. Bastin's impact on Arsenal's championship success cannot be emphasised enough – especially when one considers the fact that he was an ever-present fixture in all 42 of the north Londoners' league matches. Fellow England international David Jack also helped himself to a goal. The home team meanwhile was hovering perilously close to the relegation zone once more. A mediocre league campaign coupled with an early exit from the FA Cup persuaded the club to appoint former Arsenal manager Leslie Knighton as successor to David Calderhead.

CHELSEA	ARSENAL
1 Woodley	1 Moss
2 Barber	2 Male
3 Macaulay	3 Hapgood
4 Russell	4 Hill
5 O'Dowd	5 Roberts
6 Craig	6 John
7 Oakton	7 Jack
8 Mills	8 Bowden
9 Gallacher	9 Lambert
10 Gibson	10 James
11 Horton	11 Bastin

SEASON 1932-3:
ARSENAL:
Finished 1st; Won 25; Drew 8; Lost 9; Goals for 118; Against 61; Points 58
CHELSEA:
Finished 18th; Won 14; Drew 7; Lost 21; Goals for 63; Against 73; Points 35

ARSENAL 2 CHELSEA 1; December 16th 1933 (Crowd 43,897) Scorers: Beasley (2); Miller

With only three wins and two draws from their first seventeen outings the away team seemed to be relegation certainties. It therefore came as something of a surprise that they restricted the Gunners to the narrowest of victories. Harold 'Dusty' Miller found the target for the visitors but a double from Pat Beasley enabled Arsenal to collect both points. As the north Londoners continued to make progress towards retaining their league trophy, tragedy occurred the following month when the inspirational boss at Highbury Herbert Chapman died suddenly. This match therefore was his last taste of victory against the Blues. However, even in Chapman's absence, the Gunners maintained their superiority over Chelsea – and everyone else for that matter!

ARSENAL	CHELSEA
1 Moss	1 Woodley
2 Male	2 Odell
3 Hapgood	3 Law
4 Jones	4 Allum

5 Roberts	5 O'Dowd
6 John	6 Miller
7 Birkett	7 Oakton
8 Bastin	8 Priestley
9 Bowden	9 Mills
10 James	10 Gregg
11 Beasley	11 Chitty

CHELSEA 2 ARSENAL 2; April 28th 1934 (Crowd 65,344) Scorers: Horton Mills; James Bastin

John Horton and George Mills maintained their fine goal scoring form from previous weeks to earn the home team a commendable draw against the best team in England. Horton and Mills had now scored fourteen goals between them in Chelsea's last eight league matches and both players were hugely influential during a run of five successive wins which rescued the Blues from the dreaded drop to the second Division. Nevertheless, Arsenal was not to be denied back-to-back League Championship titles as they secured a point courtesy of goals from Cliff Bastin (again) and Scottish international Alex James. With George Allison now at the helm the Gunners simply maintained their superiority over everyone in the country.

CHELSEA	ARSENAL
1 Woodley	1 Moss
2 Barber	2 Male
3 Macaulay	3 Hapgood
4 Russell	4 Jones
5 Craig	5 Roberts
6 Hutcheson	6 Hill

7 Oakton	7 Beasley
8 Gregg	8 Bowden
9 Mills	9 Drake
10 Gibson	10 James
11 Horton	11 Bastin

SEASON 1933-4:
ARSENAL:
Finished 1st; Won 25; Drew 9; Lost 8; Goals for 75; Against 47; Points 59
CHELSEA:
Finished 19th; Won 14; Drew 8; Lost 20; Goals for 67; Against 69; Points 36

CHELSEA 2 ARSENAL 5; November 24th 1934 (Crowd 43,419) Scorers: Macaulay Gregg; Drake (4) Hulme

Scottish international goalkeeper Johnny Jackson had to pick the ball out of the net no fewer than five times as the mighty Arsenal cruised to another emphatic triumph. Chelsea's chief tormentor was Ted Drake who helped himself to a remarkable four goals haul. A full twenty years before Drake was leading the Blues to their only League Championship title, he was intent on inflicting misery upon the west Londoners. Joe Hulme assisted Drake by contributing a goal of his own, while goals from Scotsman Robert Macaulay and Robert Gregg simply added to the goal feast without endangering Arsenal's claim to both points.

CHELSEA	ARSENAL
1 Jackson	1 Moss

2 Barber	2 Male
3 Macaulay	3 Hapgood
4 Allum	4 Hill
5 Craig	5 Roberts
6 Miller	6 Copping
7 Spence	7 Hulme
8 Argue	8 Bowden
9 Mills	9 Drake
10 Gregg	10 James
11 Barraclough	11 Bastin

ARSENAL 2 CHELSEA 2; April 6th 1935; (Crowd 54,020) Scorers: Drake L Compton (Pen); Barraclough Spence

Another goal from Ted Drake helped him towards a season's total of 42 league goals which became a record at Highbury. Leslie Compton converted from the spot as the home team headed towards their third consecutive League Championship. However, goals from Willie Barraclough and Dick Spence ensured that the visitors would claim a point. The Blues managed to reach mid-table safety but this 'achievement' pales into insignificance with Arsenal's league success which was made all the sweeter when north London neighbours Tottenham Hotspur were relegated.

ARSENAL	CHELSEA
1 Wilson	1 Woodley
2 L Compton	2 Barber
3 John	3 Macaulay
4 Crayston	4 Hutcheson
5 Roberts	5 Craig

6 Hill		6 Miller
7 Kirchen		7 Spence
8 Davidson		8 Argue
9 Drake		9 Bambrick
10 James		10 Burgess
11 Beasley		11 Barraclough

SEASON 1934-5:

ARSENAL:
Finished 1st; Won 23; Drew 12; Lost 7; Goals for 115; Against 46; Points 58
CHELSEA:
Finished 12th; Won 16; Drew 9; Lost 17; Goals for 73; Against 82; Points 41

CHELSEA 1 ARSENAL 1; October 12th 1935 (Crowd 82,905) Scorers: Bambrick; Crayston

The largest ever recorded crowd at Stamford Bridge flocked to see the mighty Arsenal held 1-1 by improving Chelsea. Northern Irish international Joe Bambrick opened up the scoring and took his season's tally to seven goals from six matches. However, Jack Crayston soon equalised for the visitors after the home team had failed to clear a corner. Although the Blues had dropped a point at home, the result was quite encouraging when one considers that the League Champions Arsenal boasted no fewer than six England internationals and one Scottish international in their team. It was a testament to the pulling power of the north Londoners that their arrival in west London should attract the highest league crowd up to that time. Five of the players in this contest turned out for the Home International the following week when England won 3-1 in Belfast against Northern Ireland. Three Gunners (Bowden, Hapgood and Male) appeared for England, while Bambrick and Mitchell (both of Chelsea) lined up for the home team.

CHELSEA	ARSENAL
1 Jackson	1 Wilson
2 O'Hare	2 Male
3 Law	3 Hapgood
4 Mitchell	4 Crayston
5 Craig	5 Roberts
6 Miller	6 Hill
7 Spence	7 Milne
8 Argue	8 Bowden
9 Bambrick	9 Drake
10 Gibson	10 James
11 Barraclough	11 Bastin

ARSENAL 1 CHELSEA 1; April 27th 1936 (Crowd 40,402) Scorers: Drake; Mills

Only half the size of the crowd at Stamford Bridge witnessed the third consecutive drawn match between London's big two. Although Chelsea had failed to beat the Gunners for the ninth successive time, they could take comfort from the fact that Arsenal had failed to beat Chelsea in a league season for the first time since 1932. The home team for their part succeeded in lifting the FA Cup for the second time in their history courtesy of a goal from the prolific Ted Drake who was also on target in this contest. Centre-forward George Mills found the back of the net as the Blues briefly narrowed the gap between the two teams during an era when the north Londoners swept all before them.

ARSENAL	CHELSEA
1 Wilson	1 Woodley
2 Male	2 Barber
3 Hapgood	3 Law
4 Crayston	4 Mitchell
5 Sidey	5 Craig
6 Copping	6 Miller
7 Hulme	7 Spence
8 Bowden	8 Burgess
9 Drake	9 Mills
10 Bastin	10 Gibson
11 Beasley	11 Oakton

SEASON 1935-6:
ARSENAL:
Finished 6th; Won 15; Drew 15; Lost 12; Goals for 78; Against 48; Points 45
CHELSEA:
Finished 8th; Won 15; Drew 13; Lost 14; Goals for 65; Against 72; Points 43

ARSENAL 4 CHELSEA 1; December 19th 1936 (Crowd 49,917) Scorers: Kirchen (2) Drake Davidson; Oakton

The reigning FA Cup holders stormed to an emphatic triumph courtesy of a double from Alf Kirchen as well as goals from Bobby Davidson and Ted Drake. The home team was clearly making a determined bid to re-capture the

League Championship, and so not even a goal from Albert Oakton was going to deny them maximum points. The visitors remained marooned in mid-table as the margin between the two London giants widened once more.

ARSENAL	CHELSEA
1 Swindin	1 Woodley
2 Male	2 O'Hare
3 L Compton	3 Barber
4 Crayston	4 Mitchell
5 Roberts	5 Craig
6 Copping	6 Weaver
7 Kirchen	7 Oakton
8 James	8 Argue
9 Drake	9 Mills
10 Davidson	10 Burgess
11 Milne	11 Barraclough

CHELSEA 2 ARSENAL 0; April 24th 1937 (Crowd 53,325) Scorer: Mills (2)

A double from centre-forward George Mills ended a goals drought in which the Blues had failed to score in their previous five matches. Mills took his season's tally to 23 goals as he pressed his claims for an international call-up. Six months later, the prolific marksman was awarded his first England cap and promptly collected a hat-trick on his debut in a home international against Northern Ireland in Belfast. Ironically, the last team that Chelsea and Mills had scored against (and beaten) were Charlton Athletic who achieved a remarkable second position in the First Division on account of Arsenal's failure to win this contest. First

Brentford last year and now south London's Charlton Athletic temporarily dislodged the Gunners as the capital's top team. This was the first time since January 1924 that the north Londoners had failed to find the back of the net against their west London rivals. Fifteen games had been played out in the interim period before on this day Vic Woodley earned a rare shut-out for a Chelsea goalkeeper against the Arsenal. This achievement compensated for Woodley's experience the previous weekend when he conceded three goals as England were beaten 3-1 in Glasgow by the 'Auld Enemy.' Also, for the sixth time in seven seasons the combined attendance figures for the league matches between Arsenal and Chelsea had exceeded the 100,000 mark – a testimony to the perceived significance of such contests.

CHELSEA	ARSENAL
1 Woodley	1 Boulton
2 Chitty	2 Male
3 Barber	3 Hapgood
4 Allum	4 Crayston
5 Craig	5 Sidey
6 Weaver	6 Copping
7 Spence	7 Nelson
8 Argue	8 Bastin
9 Mills	9 Bowden
10 Burgess	10 Davidson
11 Smale	11 D Compton

SEASON 1936-7:
ARSENAL:

Finished 3rd; Won 18; Drew 16; Lost 8; Goals for 80; Against 49; Points 52
CHELSEA:
Finished 13th; Won 14; Drew 13; Lost 15; Goals for 52; Against 55; Points 41

CHELSEA 2 ARSENAL 2; October 9th 1937 (Crowd 75,952) Scorers: Argue Mills; Kirchen (2)

The second largest-ever crowd attended this London derby and witnessed both teams share four goals. England international Alf Kirchen grabbed his second double against the Blues, while goals from Scotsman Jimmy Argue and George Mills ensured that the home team would collect a point. A better than usual start to the season had misled the Chelsea contingent into believing they were ready to challenge for league honours, but Arsenal had other ideas as events would prove. This match therefore was something of a top of the table clash which explains the huge attendance figure. In the days before computers or colour televisions, football was a major source of amusement which also helps to account for such a massive crowd.

CHELSEA	ARSENAL
1 Woodley	1 Boulton
2 O'Hare	2 L Compton
3 Barber	3 Hapgood
4 Mitchell	4 Crayston
5 Griffiths	5 Roberts
6 Weaver	6 Copping
7 Buchanan	7 Kirchen
8 Argue	8 Bowden

9 Mills
10 Burgess
11 Chitty

9 Hunt
10 Bastin
11 Milne

ARSENAL 2 CHELSEA 0; February 19th 1938 (Crowd 49,513) Scorers: Griffiths Drake

Goals from Ted Drake and Mal Griffiths helped to maintain the home team's push for the league championship. Although George Allison's outfit scored fewer goals in this season than they had accumulated in the previous year they managed to narrowly overcome Wolverhampton Wanderers in order to reach top spot for the fifth time in the 1930s. The Blues, like Arsenal, only equalled their points total for the previous season and yet they too managed to improve upon their league position of 1937. One source of concern for the away team was that they had failed for the fourteenth successive time to win at Highbury.

ARSENAL
1 Swindin
2 Male
3 Hapgood
4 Crayston
5 Joy
6 Copping
7 Griffiths
8 Jones
9 Drake
10 Carr
11 Bastin

CHELSEA
1 Woodley
2 Barkas
3 Law
4 Mayes
5 Griffiths
6 Weaver
7 Buchanan
8 Burgess
9 Mills
10 Sherborne
11 Spence

SEASON 1937-8:
ARSENAL:
Finished 1st; Won 21; Drew 10; Lost 11; Goals for 77; Against 44; Points 52
CHELSEA:
Finished 10th; Won 14; Drew 13; Lost 15; Goals for 65; Against 65; Points 41

CHELSEA 4 ARSENAL 2; October 15th 1938 (Crowd 64,443) Scorers:Burgess Mills Hanson (2); Cumner Kirchen

The Gunners were put to the sword courtesy of a double from the unfortunately named Adolf Hansen while England internationals Harry Burgess and George Mills provided the other goals. This was the third consecutive season that Mills had scored in this home fixture. The League Champions responded with goals from Horace Cumner (who was one week away from making his debut for Wales) and Alf Kirchen. For the eighth successive time, the away team was unable to win in this London derby fixture. This ought to have been a morale boosting win for the Blues, but regrettably they were unable to match this performance against the other teams in the league.

CHELSEA	ARSENAL
1 Woodley	1 Swindin
2 Barber	2 Male
3 Smith	3 Hapgood
4 Allum	4 Crayston
5 Craig	5 Joy
6 Weaver	6 Copping

7 Spence	7 Kirchen
8 Argue	8 Bastin
9 Mills	9 Drake
10 Burgess	10 Jones
11 Hanson	11 Cumner

CHELSEA 2 ARSENAL 1; January 7th (Crowd 58,095)
FA Cup 3rd Round Scorers: Argue (2); Bastin

The FA Cup draw brought the two London giants together for the third time in the decade and the west Londoners took advantage of playing at home to record a narrow win. Jimmy Argue helped himself to two goals which gave the home team something to cheer about in an otherwise mediocre season. Arsenal's Cliff Bastin became the first man from either club to score ten goals in this particular London derby but even his heroics could not prevent his team falling at the first hurdle. Arsenal too were experiencing a disappointing season.

CHELSEA	ARSENAL
1 Woodley	1 Wilson
2 O'Hare	2 Male
3 Barber	3 Hapgood
4 Mitchell	4 Crayston
5 Salmond	5 Joy
6 Weaver	6 Copping
7 Spence	7 Drake
8 Argue	8 Jones
9 Payne	9 Lewis
10 Burgess	10 Drury
11 Hanson	11 Bastin

ARSENAL 1 CHELSEA 0; February 18th 1939 (Crowd 54,510) Scorer: Bremner

The last time that these two London clubs would play each other in the 1930s was marked by a goal from Gordon Bremner which decided the outcome and earned the north Londoners instant revenge for their FA Cup exit. The Blues were once more flirting with relegation while the Gunners at least managed to retain a place in the top five of the league. Both teams would not lock horns together in a peacetime encounter for a full seven years.

ARSENAL	CHELSEA
1 Wilson	1 Woodley
2 Male	2 Barber
3 Hapgood	3 Smith
4 Pryde	4 Mitchell
5 Joy	5 Salmond
6 Copping	6 Weaver
7 Drake	7 Spence
8 Bremner	8 Payne
9 Lewis	9 Mills
10 Drury	10 Argue
11 Kirchen	11 Hanson

SEASON 1938-9:
ARSENAL:
Finished 5th; Won 19; Drew 9; Lost 14; Goals for 55; Against 41; Points 47
CHELSEA:

Finished 20th; Won 12; Drew 9; Lost 21; Goals for 64; Against 80; Points 33

CHELSEA 2 ARSENAL 1; October 26th 1946 (Crowd 56,432) Scorers: Lawton (2); Lewis

England international and prolific goal scorer Tommy Lawton netted twice to help Billy Birrell's team collect both points. It was a matter of regret for the home team that Lawton's time at Stamford Bridge was all too brief. Reg Lewis scored for the Gunners who were making a less than convincing attempt to re-assert their dominance of English football.

CHELSEA	ARSENAL
1 Robertson	1 Swindin
2 Winter	2 Scott
3 Lewis	3 Joy
4 Machin	4 Waller
5 Harris	5 L Compton
6 Macaulay	6 Jones
7 Spence	7 Nelson
8 Walker	8 Gudmundsson
9 Lawton	9 Lewis
10 Goulden	10 Curtis
11 Dolding	11 O'Flanagan

CHELSEA 1 ARSENAL 1; January 11th 1947 (Crowd 70,257) FA Cup 3rd Round Scorers: Walker; McPherson

Yet again the names of London's big two were drawn together for an FA Cup third round tussle. Another huge crowd greeted the occasion in which Scottish international Tommy Walker scored for the Blues. However, a goal from Ian McPherson ensured that George Allison's team would earn a replay which meant that both teams would have to do it all again at Highbury four days later. Not for the first time the visit of Arsenal provided Stamford Bridge with its largest crowd of the season.

CHELSEA	ARSENAL
1 Medhurst	1 Swindin
2 Winter	2 Scott
3 Bathgate	3 Barnes
4 Machin	4 Sloan
5 Steffen	5 L Compton
6 Macaulay	6 Mercer
7 Spence	7 McPherson
8 Walker	8 Lewis
9 Lawton	9 Rooke
10 Goulden	10 Jones
11 Paton	11 Logie

ARSENAL 1 CHELSEA 1; January 15th 1947 (Crowd 53,350) FA Cup 3rd Round Replay Scorers: Rooke; Lawton

For the second successive time Arsenal and Chelsea shared two goals and not even the introduction of extra-time could separate the two combatants. Goals from Tommy Lawton and Ronnie Rooke merely cancelled each other out. Replay number two was fixed for the neutral venue of White Hart Lane.

ARSENAL	CHELSEA

1 Swindin	1 Medhurst
2 Male	2 Winter
3 Barnes	3 Steffen
4 Sloan	4 Machin
5 L Compton	5 Harris
6 Mercer	6 Macaulay
7 McPherson	7 Spence
8 Lewis	8 Walker
9 Rooke	9 Lawton
10 Logie	10 Goulden
11 Curtis	11 Paton

ARSENAL 0 CHELSEA 2; January 20th 1947 (Crowd 59,590) FA Cup 3rd Round 2nd Replay Scorer: Lawton (2)

Big Tommy Lawton had clearly acquired a taste for the Gunners as he took his goals tally to five from only four matches after his double had decided this contest. The ever inconsistent Chelsea had held their resolve through five hours of football and emerged triumphant. Lawton found the net in the next round too but the Blues failed to match their performances against Arsenal, and Derby County took advantage. Once more it seemed that the west Londoners had concentrated their efforts on winning against Arsenal and neglected to raise their game for other apparently less formidable challenges.

ARSENAL	CHELSEA
1 Swindin	1 Medhurst
2 Male	2 Winter
3 Barnes	3 Steffen
4 Sloan	4 Machin

5 L Compton	5 Harris
6 Mercer	6 Macaulay
7 McPherson	7 Spence
8 Lewis	8 Walker
9 Rooke	9 Lawton
10 Jones	10 Goulden
11 Logie	11 Paton

ARSENAL 1 CHELSEA 2; March 1st 1947 (Crowd 52,606) Scorers: Rudkin; Williams Goulden (Pen)

The visitors finally recorded their first league win away to Arsenal since October 1912 courtesy of goals from Len Goulden (from the penalty spot) and Reg Williams. A goal from Tom Rudkin could not prevent an historic victory for the Blues, but even in the midst of a mediocre season the Gunners still managed to finish in a higher league position than Chelsea. The away team meanwhile could congratulate themselves on finishing the season unbeaten after five closely contested matches against the Arsenal. Both combatants finished as London's two top teams, yet neither reached a top ten position. One other statistic worthy of note was that a mere 290,000 spectators were present at the five Arsenal – Chelsea games in this season.

ARSENAL	CHELSEA
1 Swindin	1 Medhurst
2 Scott	2 Winter
3 Barnes	3 Steffen
4 Sloan	4 Machin
5 L Compton	5 Harris

6 Mercer	6 Macaulay
7 McPherson	7 Spence
8 Logie	8 Walker
9 Rooke	9 Williams
10 Jones	10 Goulden
11 Rudkin	11 Prout

SEASON 1946-7:

ARSENAL:
Finished 13th; Won 16; Drew 9; Lost 17; Goals for 72; Against 70; Points 41

CHELSEA:
Finished 15th; Won 16; Drew 7; Lost 19; Goals for 69; Against 84; Points 39

CHELSEA 0 ARSENAL 0; November 1st 1947 (Crowd 67,277)

Twenty-six derby matches between the two London rivals had come and gone since the last scoreless draw in January 1924. Fast improving Arsenal were reclaiming their reputation for being hard to score against and ultimately difficult to defeat. Their cause was helped by the fact that their tormentor from the previous season (Tommy Lawton) was about to exit Stamford Bridge in favour of Notts County. The big man's absence from this fixture perhaps explains the home team's failure to score.

CHELSEA	ARSENAL
1 Robertson	1 Swindin
2 Winter	2 Scott
3 Bathgate	3 Barnes
4 Walker	4 Macaulay

5 Harris	5 L Compton
6 Machin	6 Mercer
7 Campbell	7 Roper
8 Bowie	8 Logie
9 Armstrong	9 Lewis
10 Goulden	10 Rooke
11 McInnes	11 McPherson

ARSENAL 0 CHELSEA 2; March 20th 1948 (Crowd 56,596) Scorers: Campbell Bentley

Recent recruit to Stamford Bridge Roy Bentley became entrusted with the role of scoring goals on a regular basis vacated by the departure of Tommy Lawton. Bentley chose this visit to Highbury to open his goals account for the Blues in a career that would eventually yield 150 goals. Scotsman Bobby Campbell netted the other goal as Billy Birrell's team extended their unbeaten run against their hosts to an unprecedented seven matches. It was so typical of the west Londoners to raise their game for the challenge of Arsenal and yet sink back into mediocrity in an otherwise disappointing season. At the twentieth time of asking however the Pensioners had completed a league double of clean sheets against the Gunners. This achievement was all the more meritorious when one considers that Tom Whittaker's team merely shrugged off this minor setback as they cruised to the League Championship title. With the meanest defence in the league, the north Londoners strolled to their sixth Division One success, a feat which was due in no small part to Ronnie Rooke's total of 33 goals in this season.

ARSENAL	CHELSEA
1 Swindin	1 Medhurst
2 Scott	2 Winter
3 Barnes	3 Hughes
4 Macaulay	4 Armstrong
5 L Compton	5 Harris
6 Mercer	6 Macaulay
7 Roper	7 Dyke
8 Logie	8 Bentley
9 Rooke	9 Billington
10 Forbes	10 Walker
11 D Compton	11 Campbell

SEASON 1947-8:
ARSENAL:
Finished 1st; Won 23; Drew 13; Lost 6; Goals for 81; Against 32; Points 59
CHELSEA:
Finished 18th; Won 14; Drew 9; Lost 19; Goals for 53; Against 71; Points 37

CHELSEA 0 ARSENAL 1; October 30th 1948 (Crowd 56,476) Scorer: Rooke (Pen)

A successful spot kick from Ronnie Rooke separated the two teams in this latest instalment of their local dispute. The League Champions had finally overcome the Blues after seven failed attempts. While the visitors were attempting to defend the league title, Chelsea were once more engaged in a struggle in the bottom half of the league table.

CHELSEA	ARSENAL
1 Pickering	1 Swindin
2 Bathgate	2 Scott
3 Hughes	3 Barnes
4 Goulden	4 Macaulay
5 Harris	5 L Compton
6 Macaulay	6 Mercer
7 Dyke	7 Roper
8 Williams	8 Logie
9 Bentley	9 Rooke
10 Walker	10 Forbes
11 McInnes	11 McPherson

ARSENAL 1 CHELSEA 2; April 23rd 1949 (Crowd 58,000) Scorers: D Compton; Goulden Billington

Middlesex and England international cricketer Denis Compton may have been in the twilight of his footballing career, but he still managed to find the back of the net in this encounter. Nevertheless, goals from Hugh Billington and Len Goulden secured Chelsea's fourth successive postwar league triumph at Highbury. Although the Gunners surrendered their five months unbeaten run at home, they proceeded to win their three remaining league fixtures and finish in the top five in Division One. The visitors had little to smile about as this was their only triumph in their last eight league matches as they finished again in the wrong half of the league.

ARSENAL	CHELSEA
1 Swindin	1 Medhurst
2 Barnes	2 Winter
3 Smith	3 Hughes

4 Macaulay	4 Armstrong
5 L Compton	5 Harris
6 Forbes	6 Macaulay
7 McPherson	7 Campbell
8 Logie	8 Billington
9 Lewis	9 Bentley
10 Lishman	10 Goulden
11 D Compton	11 McInnes

SEASON 1948-9:
ARSENAL:
Finished 5th; Won 18; Drew 13; Lost 11; Goals for 74; Against 44; Points 49
CHELSEA:
Finished 13th; Won 12; Drew 14; Lost 16; Goals for 60; Against 68; Points 38

CHELSEA 1 ARSENAL 2; August 24th 1949 (Crowd 63,196) Scorers: Harris (Pen); Lishman Goring

Scotsman John Harris converted from the penalty spot, but his effort could not halt Arsenal's march toward maximum points. Peter Goring and Doug Lishman both found the target for the visitors whose arrival in west London would provide Stamford Bridge with its largest league crowd of the season. The home team would have the opportunity the following week to avenge this defeat.

CHELSEA	ARSENAL
1 Medhurst	1 Swindin
2 Winter	2 Barnes
3 Hughes	3 Smith

4 Armstrong	4 Macaulay
5 Harris	5 Daniel
6 Mitchell	6 Forbes
7 Campbell	7 McPherson
8 Goulden	8 Logie
9 Bentley	9 Goring
10 Williams	10 Lishman
11 Jones	11 Roper

ARSENAL 2 CHELSEA 3 August 31st 1949 (Crowd 52,901) Scorers: Goring(2); Billington(2) Bentley

Roy Bentley's third goal in four games was an indication that the England international intended to maintain the goalscoring momentum of his previous season when he netted twenty-three times. However his efforts were overshadowed by a double from Hugh Billington, while Peter Goring weighed in with a brace of goals for the hosts. Having scored three times in these two August derby matches Peter Goring was well on his way to a league total of 21 goals which would be the fourth highest in 1950, but he could not halt the bizarre statistic that for the ninth successive time this particular London derby, proved unfruitful for the home team. Full-back Stan Willemse made his debut for the west Londoners on this day.

ARSENAL	CHELSEA
1 Swindin	1 Medhurst
2 Scott	2 Winter
3 Barnes	3 Willemse

4 Mercer	4 Armstrong
5 L Compton	5 Harris
6 Shaw	6 Mitchell
7 McPherson	7 Campbell
8 Logie	8 Goulden
9 Goring	9 Bentley
10 Lishman	10 Billington
11 Roper	11 Gray

ARSENAL 2 CHELSEA 2; March 18th 1950 (Crowd 67,752) FA Cup Semi-Final Scorers: Cox L Compton; Bentley (2)

In the twenty years since Arsenal's last victory over Chelsea in an FA Cup contest, they had failed five times to defeat the west Londoners. Brought together to do battle at the semi-finals stage, the two London giants proceeded to serve up an epic dish of drama. Roy Bentley pressed his claim for a place in the England World Cup Finals team by scoring twice to provide the Pensioners with a seemingly unassailable lead. Having lobbed George Swindin and then heading home a Billy Hughes cross ten minutes before half-time, Bentley had put the Blues within reach of their first peacetime FA Cup Final. However, the clash was transformed when Freddie Cox scored direct from a corner kick shortly before half-time. Revitalised Arsenal were rewarded with a replay courtesy of another goal from a corner when Leslie Compton went forward to head his brother's corner into the net. The Gunners had chances to then win the game in the last quarter of an hour but had to settle for a re-match again at White Hart Lane in four days time. Refusing to lie down and accept defeat would become a recurring theme of Arsenal's struggles with Chelsea.

ARSENAL	CHELSEA
1 Swindin	1 Medhurst
2 Scott	2 Winter
3 Barnes	3 Hughes
4 Forbes	4 Armstrong
5 L Compton	5 Harris
6 Mercer	6 Mitchell
7 Cox	7 Gray
8 Logie	8 Goulden
9 Goring	9 Bentley
10 Lewis	10 Billington
11 D Compton	11 Williams

ARSENAL 1 CHELSEA 0; March 22nd 1950 (Crowd 65,482) FA Cup Semi-Final Replay Scorer: Cox

It took the introduction of extra-time to separate the two London rivals after the stalemate had exceeded the three hour mark. A decade and a half before substitutes were first used, both sets of players had to struggle on in the second part of their marathon encounter. Eventually, the deadlock was broken by a special goal when Freddie Cox embarked on a solo run to the edge of the Chelsea penalty area before unleashing the decisive blow. A Lewis double in the final would hand the Gunners their third FA Cup success. The north Londoners would once again end the league season as the capital's top team, but a fresh challenge from newly-promoted Tottenham Hotspur was on the horizon.

ARSENAL	CHELSEA
1 Swindin	1 Medhurst
2 Scott	2 Winter
3 Barnes	3 Hughes
4 Macaulay	4 Armstrong
5 L Compton	5 Harris
6 Mercer	6 Mitchell
7 Cox	7 Campbell
8 Logie	8 Goulden
9 Goring	9 Bentley
10 Lewis	10 Williams
11 D Compton	11 Gray

SEASON 1949-50:
ARSENAL:
Finished 6th; Won 19; Drew 11; Lost 12; Goals for 79; Against 55; Points 49
CHELSEA:
Finished 13th; Won 12; Drew 16; Lost 14; Goals for 58; Against 65; Points 40

ARSENAL 0 CHELSEA 0; August 25th 1950 (Crowd 61,166)

Highbury's first league fixture of the season ended in a no-score draw as the visitors restricted the FA Cup holders to a solitary point, thus prolonging their unbeaten post-war record at Arsenal.

ARSENAL	CHELSEA
1 Swindin	1 Medhurst

2 Barnes	2 Bathgate
3 Smith	3 Willemse
4 Forbes	4 Armstrong
5 L Compton	5 Harris
6 Mercer	6 Mitchell
7 Cox	7 Gray
8 Logie	8 Bowie
9 Goring	9 Bentley
10 Lishman	10 Billington
11 Roper	11 Williams

CHELSEA 0 ARSENAL 1; August 30th 1950 (Crowd 48,792) Scorer: Cox

Five months after scoring the decisive goal in the FA Cup semi-final replay, Freddie Cox was Chelsea's tormentor again. The Blues had now failed to score in three of their first four league matches, which was an ominous sign for another near disastrous campaign in which relegation was only narrowly averted by four straight wins in the west Londoners' last four outings. Once more the jinx that had plagued home teams in this London derby in the immediate post-war years had reared its ugly head. This was after all Arsenal's third consecutive win at Stamford Bridge and eleven games had now come and gone since either team managed to beat the other on home soil. This was the first time in 26 years that the Gunners had managed to collect two shut-outs in a league season against their west London rivals. Nevertheless, the away team's final top five league position was ruined by the emergence of Tottenham Hotspur as not only London's premier team, but as the new league champions only twelve months after they had won the Second Division title.

CHELSEA	ARSENAL
1 Medhurst	1 Swindin
2 Bathgate	2 Barnes
3 Willemse	3 Smith
4 Armstrong	4 Shaw
5 Harris	5 L Compton
6 Mitchell	6 Mercer
7 Gray	7 Cox
8 Bowie	8 Logie
9 Bentley	9 Goring
10 Billington	10 Lishman
11 Campbell	11 McPherson

SEASON 1950-1:
ARSENAL:
Finished 5th; Won 19; Drew 9; Lost 14; Goals for 73; Against 56; Points 47
CHELSEA:
Finished 20th; Won 12; Drew 8; Lost 22; Goals for 53; Against 65; Points 32

CHELSEA 1 ARSENAL 3; August 22nd 1951 (crowd 59,143) Scorers: Campbell; Holton Marden Roper

Goals from Cliff Holton, Ben Marden, and Don Roper provided the away team with their fourth successive triumph at Stamford Bridge. Bobby Campbell found the target for the Blues, but it could not prevent Arsenal stretching their unbeaten run at this venue to six league and cup matches. The largest crowd at west London in this season had witnessed the last league match that Billy Birrell would host as Chelsea manager against the visiting Gunners. Nevertheless, the home team still harboured hopes of prolonging the away team ascendancy in these fixtures when they planned their proposed visit to Highbury in one week's time.

CHELSEA	ARSENAL
1 Robertson	1 Swindin
2 Bathgate	2 Scott
3 Tickridge	3 Barnes
4 McKnight	4 Forbes
5 Saunders	5 Daniel
6 Dickson	6 Mercer
7 Parsons	7 Roper
8 Campbell	8 Logie
9 Smith	9 Holton
10 Armstrong	10 Lishman
11 Gray	11 Marden

ARSENAL 2 CHELSEA 1; August 29th 1951 (Crowd 48,768) Scorers: Holton Lishman; Smith

Not even a goal from future Spurs star Bobby Smith could stop the home team recording their first league double in this local feud since 1933. Cliff Holton and Doug Lishman were responsible for the goals which ensured Arsenal's first home victory against the Pensioners since February 1939. Chelsea's third consecutive league defeat paved the way for another year of struggle. The visitors' Reg Williams was forced to retire through injury after this contest while

Arsenal's Lawrence Scott also played his last game for the Gunners in this match.

ARSENAL	CHELSEA
1 Swindin	1 Robertson
2 Scott	2 Bathgate
3 Barnes	3 Tickridge
4 Forbes	4 Williams
5 Daniel	5 Saunders
6 Mercer	6 Dickson
7 Roper	7 Parsons
8 Logie	8 Campbell
9 Holton	9 Smith
10 Lishman	10 Armstrong
11 Marden	11 Gray

ARSENAL 1 CHELSEA 1; April 5th 1952 (Crowd 68,084)
FA Cup Semi-Final Scorers: Cox; Gray

This cup match was played peculiarly on the same day as a Home International clash at Hampden Park between the 'Auld Enemies' which Scotland won 2-1. Anyhow, at White Hart Lane another big crowd witnessed another drawn encounter between the Blues and the Gunners. Freddie Cox found the back of Chelsea's net once more, but with Billy Gray scoring for the west Londoners, a replay was required yet again to separate the seemingly inseparable.

ARSENAL	CHELSEA
1 Swindin	1 Robertson

2 Barnes	2 Bathgate
3 L Smith	3 Tickridge
4 Forbes	4 Armstrong
5 Daniel	5 Harris
6 Mercer	6 Dickson
7 Cox	7 J Smith
8 Logie	8 D'Arcy
9 Lewis	9 R Smith
10 Lishman	10 Bentley
11 Roper	11 Gray

ARSENAL 3 CHELSEA 0; April 7th 1952 (Crowd 57,450)
FA Cup Semi-Final Replay Scorers: Cox (2) Lishman

Unlike their cup duels in 1947 and in 1950 the two combatants did not need extra time on this occasion to determine the outcome. Doug Lishman netted his 25th goal of the season, but it was Freddie Cox who stole the show by scoring twice and sinking the Pensioners for the second time in three years. Blues' Manger Billy Birrell would step aside at the end of this season on the back of eight successive failures to overcome the north Londoners. It was however not all wine and roses for Arsenal because they only secured two wins in their eight remaining fixtures, and therefore ended up losing another cup final against Newcastle as well as being pipped for second place in the league by their neighbours Tottenham Hotspur.

ARSENAL	CHELSEA
1 Swindin	1 Robertson
2 Barnes	2 Bathgate
3 L Smith	3 Tickridge

4 Forbes	4 Armstrong
5 Daniel	5 Harris
6 Mercer	6 Dickson
7 Cox	7 J Smith
8 Logie	8 D'Arcy
9 Goring	9 R Smith
10 Lishman	10 Bentley
11 Roper	11 Gray

SEASON 1951-2:
ARSENAL:
Finished 3rd; Won 21; Drew 11; Lost 10; Goals for 80; Against 61; Points 53
CHELSEA:
Finished 19th; Won 14; Drew 8; Lost 20; Goals for 52; Against 72; Points 36
CHELSEA 1 ARSENAL 1; April 3rd 1953 (Crowd 72,614)
Scorers: Parsons; Goring

The largest crowd at Stamford Bridge for four and a half years were present to see the points shared. Eric Parsons found the back of the net for the home team but Peter Goring's goal kept the visitors on course for another possible league title. Former Arsenal and England centre-forward Ted Drake was now entrusted with the task of transforming the Blues from under-achievers to trophy hunters and although his first match against his former club ended in an honourable draw, both teams remained poles apart in terms of league positions. Arsenal's lucky mascot in these derby matches Freddie Cox played out his last league match fittingly against Chelsea.

CHELSEA	ARSENAL
1 Thomson	1 Kelsey
2 Harris	2 Wade
3 Willemse	3 Smith
4 Armstrong	4 Shaw
5 Greenwood	5 Daniel
6 Dickson	6 Forbes
7 Parsons	7 Cox
8 McNichol	8 Logie
9 Lewis	9 Goring
10 Edwards	10 Lishman
11 Blunstone	11 Roper

ARSENAL 2 CHELSEA 0; April 6th 1953 (Crowd 40,536)
Scorers: Lishman Marden

Seventy-two hours after the stalemate in west London, the Gunners extended their unbeaten run against Chelsea to ten league and cup matches. Prolific scorer Doug Lishman added one to his season's tally en route to a total of 25 goals, while Ben Marden also found the target. The north Londoners had no fewer than eight league commitments during the month of April, but this massive burden could not prevent Tom Whittaker's team sneaking home for their second post-war league championship. As for the Blues, merely staying in the First Division appeared to remain the extent of their footballing ambitions. Chelsea duo Billy Gray and Sid Tickridge competed for the last time in a Blues shirt on this day.

ARSENAL	CHELSEA
1 Swindin	1 Thomson

2 Wade	2 Tickridge
3 Smith	3 Willemse
4 Forbes	4 Armstrong
5 Daniel	5 Greenwood
6 Mercer	6 Harris
7 Roper	7 Gray
8 Logie	8 Bentley
9 Goring	9 Lewis
10 Lishman	10 McNichol
11 Marden	11 Blunstone

SEASON 1952-3:
ARSENAL:
Finished 1st; Won 21; Drew 12; Lost 9; Goals for 97; Against 64; Points 54
CHELSEA:
Finished 19th; Won 12; Drew 11; Lost 19; Goals for 56; Against 66; Points 35

ARSENAL 1 CHELSEA 2; September 8th 1953 (Crowd 55,086) Scorers: Holton; Bentley Lewis

Ted Drake's mission to cast aside Chelsea's image as also-rans was given a boost with this encouraging win at Highbury. England international Roy Bentley and Jim Lewis scored the goals which helped sink Arsenal for the first time since August 1949. Not even a goal from Cliff Holton could rescue the Gunners from their fifth defeat from their first seven league matches. Remarkably, the reigning league champions found themselves bottom of the First Division after a wretched start to the new league season. Inside-forwards Leonard Kell and Peter Tiller made their debut appearances in this fixture.

ARSENAL	CHELSEA
1 Swindin	1 Robertson
2 Barnes	2 Harris
3 Smith	3 Willemse
4 Forbes	4 Armstrong
5 Dodgin	5 F Saunders
6 Bowen	6 D Saunders
7 Milton	7 Bentley
8 Logie	8 McNichol
9 Holton	9 Lewis
10 Tilley	10 Kell
11 Roper	11 Blunstone

CHELSEA 0 ARSENAL 2; September 15th 1953 (Crowd 60,652) Scorer: Lishman (2)

Stamford Bridge's second largest crowd of the season witnessed a double from Doug Lishman that presented the away team with revenge for their home defeat one week earlier. Of more significance was the fact that the League Champions had recorded their first league triumph at the ninth attempt. This morale boosting victory came only three days after the mighty Arsenal had been thumped 7-1 at Sunderland. Eventually, the north Londoners managed to haul themselves up to a mid-table position which was an achievement in itself, but this was eclipsed by Chelsea's first post-war finish in the top ten as the Blues finished above Arsenal as London's top team for the first time since 1922.

CHELSEA	ARSENAL
1 Robertson	1 Kelsey
2 Harris	2 Wade
3 Willemse	3 Barnes
4 Armstrong	4 Shaw
5 Greenwood	5 Dodgin
6 D Saunders	6 Bowen
7 Bentley	7 Forbes
8 Smith	8 Logie
9 Lewis	9 Holton
10 McNichol	10 Lishman
11 Blunstone	11 Roper

SEASON 1953-4:
CHELSEA:
Finished 8th; Won 16; Drew 12; Lost 14; Goals for 74; Against 68; Points 44
ARSENAL:
Finished 12th; Won 15; Drew 13; Lost 14; Goals for 75; Against 73; Points 43

ARSENAL 1 CHELSEA 0; December 25th 1954 (Crowd 47,178) Scorer: Lawton
Former Blues' favourite Tommy Lawton returned to this fixture to haunt his former employers with the only goal of this Christmas Day game. The north Londoners were experiencing another below average start to their league campaign but at least they had brought a run of four successive wins by Chelsea to an end. The away team were intent on retaining their new-found status as London's top team as they prepared to do battle with their

rivals in two days' time. They would do so without centre-half Ron Greenwood who played his last match for the west Londoners in this contest.

ARSENAL
1 Kelsey
2 Barnes
3 Evans
4 Goring
5 Fotheringham
6 Bowen
7 Clapton
8 Tapscott
9 Lawton
10 Lishman
11 Haverty

CHELSEA
1 Robertson
2 Harris
3 Willemse
4 Armstrong
5 Greenwood
6 Saunders
7 Parsons
8 McNichol
9 Bentley
10 Stubbs
11 Blunstone

CHELSEA 1 ARSENAL 1; December 27th 1954 (Crowd 66,922) Scorers: O'Connell; Tapscott

Amateur centre-forward Seamus O'Connell found the back of the net for the home team, but a goal from Derek Tapscott ensured that the visitors would obtain a point. It was a case of roles reversed as the Gunners put extra effort into overcoming the Blues while Chelsea's ambitions extended towards an elusive League Championship title.Although the west Londoners had enjoyed a better than usual first half of the season, few observers from the large crowd assembled at this contest would have believed that Drake's ducklings were on course for the club's first (and only) League Championship success. For once, mid-table Arsenal were left trailing in Chelsea's wake.

CHELSEA	ARSENAL
1 Robertson	1 Kelsey
2 Sillett	2 Barnes
3 Willemse	3 Evans
4 Armstrong	4 Goring
5 Wicks	5 Fotheringham
6 Saunders	6 Bowen
7 Parsons	7 Clapton
8 McNichol	8 Tapscott
9 Bentley	9 Lawton
10 O'Connell	10 Lishman
11 Blunstone	11 Haverty

SEASON 1954-5:
CHELSEA:
Finished 1st; Won 20; Drew 12; Lost 10; Goals for 81; Against 57; Points 52
ARSENAL:
Finished 9th; Won 17; Drew 9; Lost 16; Goals for 69; Against 63; Points 43

ARSENAL 1 CHELSEA 1: August 27th 1955 (Crowd 56,034) Scorers: Lawton; O'Connell

Veteran goal scorer Tommy Lawton left his mark on another derby match while Seamus O'Connell was relied upon to secure a point for the reigning League Champions. Both teams had only won one of their first three league matches, so there was little evidence to suggest that either outfit was likely to mount a prolonged challenge for league honours.

ARSENAL	CHELSEA
1 Kelsey	1 Thomson
2 Barnes	2 Sillett
3 Evans	3 Willemse
4 Goring	4 Armstrong
5 Fotheringham	5 Wicks
6 Bowen	6 Saunders
7 Clapton	7 Parsons
8 Tapscott	8 McNichol
9 Lawton	9 Bentley
10 Lishman	10 O'Connell
11 Roper	11 Blunstone

CHELSEA 2 ARSENAL 0; December 24th 1955 Crowd (43,022) Scorers: Bentley Blunstone

Arsenal's impressive run of form at Stamford Bridge finally came to an end in this Christmas Eve game. Goals from England internationals Roy Bentley and Frank Blunstone secured Chelsea's first home win against the Gunners since October 1946. This win also kept the Blues ahead of the north Londoners in the league, but an excellent finish to the season saw Arsenal overtake their London rivals and re-gain their position as London's top club. Chelsea's ascendancy had been short-lived. Arsenal full-back Stan Charlton made his league debut in this contest which proved to be the last Chelsea fixture commitment for the admirable Tom Whittaker who died in October 1956.

CHELSEA	ARSENAL
1 Robertson	1 Sullivan
2 Sillett	2 Charlton
3 Willemse	3 Evans
4 Armstrong	4 Goring
5 Wicks	5 Fotheringham
6 Saunders	6 Holton
7 Parsons	7 Clapton
8 McNichol	8 Tapscott
9 Bentley	9 Groves
10 Stubbs	10 Bloomfield
11 Blunstone	11 Tiddy

SEASON 1955-6:
ARSENAL:
Finished 5th; Won 18; Drew 10; Lost 14; Goals for 60; Against 61; Points 46
CHELSEA:
Finished 16th; Won 14; Drew 11; Lost 17; Goals for 64; Against 77; Points 39

CHELSEA 1 ARSENAL 1: December 25th 1956 (Crowd 34,094) Scorers: McNichol; Bloomfield

The visitors' new manager Jack Crayston was no stranger to such derby fixtures as both he and his opposite number Ted Drake had both played and scored in contests for Arsenal against the Blues a couple of decades earlier. On this occasion, both clubs entered into the festive spirit by presenting each other with a goal and a point. Chief beneficiaries of such generosity were Jimmy Bloomfield and Johnny McNichol who each grabbed a goal. More than thirty thousand people temporarily abandoned their Christmas Day celebrations to witness this clash.

CHELSEA	ARSENAL
1 Matthews	1 Sullivan
2 MacFarlane	2 Charlton
3 Sillett	3 Evans
4 Mortimore	4 Holton
5 Livingstone	5 Dodgin
6 Saunders	6 Bowen
7 Brabrook	7 Clapton
8 McNichol	8 Tapscott
9 Tindall	9 Herd
10 Nicholas	10 Bloomfield
11 Blunstone	11 Haverty

ARSENAL 2 CHELSEA 0; December 26th 1956 (Crowd 22,526) Scorers: Clapton Tapscott

24 hours later and the Gunners were in no mood for generosity as they brushed the Blues aside 2-0. An abnormally low turnout greeted this Boxing Day game and it came as no surprise that such back-to-back clashes over Christmas would not be repeated in future years as the attendance figures were half what they otherwise might have been. Danny Clapton who made his debut in this derby fixture on Christmas Day 1954 celebrated his second anniversary with the Gunners by finding the back of the net. Derek Tapscott also found the target as he had done on December 27th 1954. It proved to be a season of mixed fortunes for both London rivals; Chelsea improved their league position from the previous season while Arsenal

held on to their top five position. However, such progress was eclipsed by their neighbours Tottenham Hotspur whose second place finish rendered them the capital's top team once again.

ARSENAL	CHELSEA
1 Kelsey	1 Matthews
2 Charlton	2 MacFarlane
3 Evans	3 Sillett
4 Holton	4 Armstrong
5 Dodgin	5 Livingstone
6 Bowen	6 Saunders
7 Clapton	7 Brabrook
8 Tapscott	8 McNichol
9 Herd	9 Lewis
10 Bloomfield	10 Stubbs
11 Haverty	11 Blunstone

SEASON 1956-7:
ARSENAL:
Finished 5th; Won 21; Drew 8; Lost 13; Goals for 85; Against 69; Points 50
CHELSEA:
Finished 12th; Won 13; Drew 13; Lost 16; Goals for 73; Against 73; Points 39
CHELSEA 0 ARSENAL 0; October 26th 1957 (Crowd 66,007)

It was a pity that Stamford Bridge's largest crowd for two and a half years should be treated to a rare no scoring draw between the two protagonists. The lack of goals was all the more surprising when one considers that a certain Mr Jimmy Greaves was now playing for the Blues. Having failed to sufficiently entertain west London's biggest gathering of this season, both teams made amends in the next match between them in the following spring when they served up a goals feast.

CHELSEA	ARSENAL
1 Matthews	1 Kelsey
2 Whittaker	2 Charlton
3 Sillett	3 Evans
4 B Nicholas	4 Goring
5 Mortimore	5 Dodgin
6 Saunders	6 Wills
7 Brabrook	7 Clapton
8 Greaves	8 Tapscott
9 Tindall	9 Holton
10 A. Nicholas	10 Bloomfield
11 Block	11 Haverty

ARSENAL 5 CHELSEA 4; March 8th 1958 (Crowd 41,570) Scorers: Herd (3) Clapton Bloomfield; Tindall Greaves (2) Block

Both London rivals have not always done justice to the huge masses of people who swelled the ranks whenever the two neighbours locked horns together. However, on this day, nobody could have cause to complain about the action that unfolded. It is probably fair to say that each manager was less than satisfied with his defence. Nevertheless, six men helped themselves to goals, thereby producing the first and only occasion when more than seven goals were netted in a contest between the two teams. Michael Block, Jimmy Bloomfield, Danny Clapton and Ron Tindall each shared a goal whilst Chelsea's new goalscoring hero Jimmy Greaves went one better. However, even his efforts were eclipsed by another young centre-forward David Herd who stole the show⁻ with a hat trick. One consolation for the Blues would be their position above Arsenal at the end of the season, but it was Tottenham Hotspur who emerged as London's top team for the second successive year.

ARSENAL	CHELSEA
1 Kelsey	1 Matthews
2 Charlton	2 Sillett
3 Wills	3 MacFarlane
4 Ward	4 Mortimore
5 Fotheringham	5 Livingstone
6 Petts	6 Casey
7 Clapton	7 Brabrook
8 Groves	8 Cliss
9 Herd	9 Tindall
10 Bloomfield	10 Greaves
11 Nutt	11 Block

SEASON 1957-8:
CHELSEA:
Finished 11th; Won 15; Drew 12; Lost 15; Goals for 83; Against 79; Points 42
ARSENAL:
Finished 12th; Won 16; Drew 7; Lost 19; Goals for 73; Against 85; Points 39
CHELSEA 0 ARSENAL 3; November 22nd 1958 (Crowd 57,910) Scorers: Henderson Clapton Barnwell

Eighteen months after his first and only league appearance for the visitors John Barnwell celebrated his long-awaited second outing by finding the back of the Chelsea net. Stamford Bridge's third largest crowd of the season witnessed another goal from Danny Clapton while Jackie Henderson also found the target five weeks after he collected the first of two caps for Scotland. Whilst the home team remained anchored in mid-table, the Gunners were making a renewed attempt to win back the league.

CHELSEA	ARSENAL
1 Matthews	1 Kelsey
2 P Sillett	2 Wills
3 J Sillett	3 Evans
4 Huxford	4 Docherty
5 Scott	5 Dodgin
6 Saunders	6 Bowen
7 Brabrook	7 Clapton
8 Greaves	8 Barnwell
9 Tindall	9 Henderson
10 Nicholas	10 Bloomfield
11 Harrison	11 Haverty

ARSENAL 1 CHELSEA 1; April 11th 1959 (Crowd 40,900) Scorers: Ward; Greaves

On the same day that England were narrowly overcoming Scotland at Wembley, Arsenal was failing for the sixth successive time to win a league match. Gerald Ward's goal was cancelled out by the prolific Jimmy Greaves who ended the season as the joint highest goalscorer in the First

Division. One dreads to think how the mediocre away team could have coped without the exceptional Greaves. Meanwhile, the wheels had well and truly come off Arsenal's league challenge, but three wins in their last three contests helped them to a top three spot. The west Londoners would have craved such a lofty position.

ARSENAL	CHELSEA
1 Standen	1 Matthews
2 Evans	2 P Sillett
3 McCullough	3 Whittaker
4 Ward	4 Anderton
5 Dodgin	5 Mortimore
6 Bowen	6 Crowther
7 Henderson	7 Brabrook
8 Groves	8 Greaves
9 Julians	9 allen
10 Barnwell	10 Blunstone
11 Haverty	11 Harrison

SEASON 1958-9:
ARSENAL:
Finished 3rd; Won 21; Drew 8; Lost 13; Goals for 88; Against 68; Points 50
CHELSEA:
Finished 14th; Won 18; Drew 4; Lost 20; Goals for 77; Against 98; Points 40

CHELSEA 1 ARSENAL 3; November 21st 1959 (Crowd 52,738) Scorers: Gibbs; Haverty (2) Bloomfield

The last derby match between these two London clubs in the 1950s saw the Gunners extend their unbeaten run against the Blues to seven games. Derek Gibbs scored one of his rare goals for the home team, but the Arsenal were not to be denied both points. Jimmy Bloomfield was on target for the visitors but his effort was overshadowed by a double from Republic of Ireland international Joe Haverty. After losing only one of their first ten league matches, the north Londoners seemed poised for a prolonged league challenge, but only one win in their last seven league encounters meant that George Swindin's team were rubbing shoulders with the home team in the wrong half of the league table. Meanwhile, Peter Corthine played the last of his two appearances for Chelsea in this contest before moving on to Southend. Having each won the First Division in this decade both teams were not exactly bowing out of the 1950s in style.

CHELSEA	ARSENAL
1 Matthews	1 Kelsey
2 Shellito	2 Wills
3 P Sillett	3 McCullough
4 Anderton	4 Groves
5 Mortimore	5 Dodgin
6 Crowther	6 Petts
7 Corthine	7 Clapton
8 Greaves	8 Barnwell
9 Livesey	9 Henderson
10 Gibbs	10 Bloomfield
11 Blunstone	11 Haverty

ARSENAL 1 CHELSEA 4: April 9th 1960 (Crowd 40,700)
Scorers: Bloomfield; P Sillett (Pen) Brabrook (2) Brooks

Despite another goal from Jimmy Bloomfield, the away team ended their seven year Highbury hoodoo in emphatic fashion. Chief destroyer was England international Peter Brabrook who netted twice, while John Brooks and Peter Sillett from the spot also converted a goal each. Big Bill Dodgin made his last league appearance for the Gunners after almost ten years at Highbury. Although Jimmy Greaves finished the season as the First Division's joint second highest goalscorer, Drake's ducklings were struggling to stay afloat in Division One. As for the north Londoners, three further defeats in their last four league matches completed a miserable campaign which found them only third in the capital's pecking order – behind fast improving Tottenham Hotspur and Fulham.

ARSENAL	CHELSEA
1 Kelsey	1 Bonetti
2 Magill	2 J Sillett
3 McCullough	3 P Sillett
4 Docherty	4 Anderton
5 Dodgin	5 Mortimore
6 Groves	6 Crowther
7 Henderson	7 Brabrook
8 Barnwell	8 Greaves
9 Herd	9 Tindall
10 Bloomfield	10 Brooks
11 Haverty	11 Blunstone

SEASON 1959-60:

ARSENAL:
Finished 13th; Won 15; Drew 9; Lost 18; Goals for 68; Against 80; Points 39
CHELSEA:
Finished 18th; Won 14; Drew 9; Lost 19; Goals for 76; Against 91; Points 37

ARSENAL 1 CHELSEA 4: November 12th 1960 (Crowd 38,886) Scorers: Charles; Greaves Tambling Mortimore Tindall

Eleven days before netting twice for England at Wembley in a 5-1 thumping of Wales, Jimmy Greaves was amongst the scorers as the away team remarkably repeated their crushing defeat of seven months earlier. Not even a goal from Mel Charles could stem the west London tidal wave as John Mortimore, young Bobby Tambling and Ron Tindall all proceeded to find the back of Jack Kelsey's net. It was the Arsenal goalkeeper who had to pick the ball five times out of the net when his Welsh team were annihilated by Greaves and company the following week. This match proved to be Ted Drake's last visit as Chelsea manager to his old stamping ground. How appropriate that it should end in a resounding triumph for the former Arsenal centre-forward.

ARSENAL	CHELSEA
1 Kelsey	1 Bonetti
2 Wills	2 P Sillett
3 McCullough	3 A Harris
4 Docherty	4 Venables
5 Snedden	5 Evans

6 Groves	6 Mortimore
7 Strong	7 Brabrook
8 Barnwell	8 Greaves
9 Charles	9 Tindall
10 Herd	10 Brooks
11 Henderson	11 Tambling

CHELSEA 3 ARSENAL 1; April 15th 1961 (Crowd 38,233) Scorers: Tambling Tindall Neill (OG); Strong
For many English football observers, this day in April comes second only to the World Cup Final in 1966 as the highlight of English soccer. This date is not cherished because it was the first time since 1947 that Chelsea had recorded a league double over Arsenal, but because across London, at Wembley, the host nation were humiliating Scotland to the tune of nine goals to three! A certain Jimmy Greaves was contributing no less than three goals to that annihilation. Meanwhile at Stamford Bridge, his team-mates were able to cope with his enforced absence by inflicting their third consecutive defeat on the Gunners. Not even a goal from Geoff Strong was going to stop this Chelsea outfit creating their own piece of history by registering the west London club's first ever sequence of three consecutive peacetime triumphs against their north London neighbours. Northern Irishman Terry Neill contributed to this historic victory by putting the ball into his own net. The fast improving Bobby Tambling and Ron Tindall bagged the home team's other goals. Having been between the sticks when Chelsea recorded their double in 1947 the unfortunate George Swindin was now Arsenal manager when this achievement was repeated fourteen years later. This would be the first of three crushing defeats

inflicted on his troops as the curtains came down on another disappointing league season for Arsenal. At least they still finished in a loftier position than the Blues in spite of their recent defeats at the hands of the west London club. What really ruined the football season for many Arsenal supporters was a remarkable league and cup double for their north London neighbours Tottenham Hotspur. This league match was also the last derby match between two of London's finest that Ted Drake was involved in.A bad start to the following season saw Drake obliged to vacate the manager's chair in favour of former Arsenal defender Tommy Docherty. It was a matter of irony that just as Chelsea were starting to get the better of Arsenal that Drake should be asked to step down.

CHELSEA	ARSENAL
1 Bonetti	1 Kelsey
2 J Sillett	2 Bacuzzi
3 P Sillett	3 McCullough
4 Bradbury	4 Charles
5 Scott	5 Neill
6 Anderton	6 Groves
7 Blunstone	7 Strong
8 Brooks	8 Barnwell
9 Tindall	9 Herd
10 Tambling	10 Eastham
11 Harrison	11 Henderson

SEASON 1960-1:
ARSENAL:
Finished 11th; Won 15; Drew 11; Lost 16; Goals for 77; Against 85; Points 41

CHELSEA:
Finished 12th; Won 15; Drew 7; Lost 20; Goals for 98;
Against 100; Points 37

ARSENAL 0 CHELSEA 3; November 4th 1961 (Crowd
37,604) Scorers: Blunstone Bridges (2)

Former West Ham stalwart Andrew Malcolm made a happy
debut for the visitors as the Blues cruised to an
unprecedented fourth emphatic victory in succession over
the Gunners. New Chelsea player-coach Tommy Docherty
was back on familiar ground where he saw his struggling
team record their first triumph under his stewardship
courtesy of a double from young Barry Bridges as well as
another derby goal from England international Frank
Blunstone. In a league season in which the west Londoners
ended up conceding more goals than any other team in the
top flight, the failure of Arsenal to find the back of the net
was a welcome boost for goalkeeper Peter Bonetti and his
defence.

ARSENAL	CHELSEA
1 Kelsey	1 Bonetti
2 Magill	2 Shellito
3 McCullough	3 A Harris
4 Ward	4 Malcolm
5 Brown	5 Scott
6 Groves	6 Bradbury
7 MacLeod	7 Murray
8 Barnwell	8 Tambling
9 Charles	9 Brabrook
10 Eastham	10 Bridges

11 Skirton   11 Blunstone

CHELSEA 2 ARSENAL 3: March 24th 1962 (Crowd 31,016) Scorers: Brabrook Harrison; Skirton Barnwell MacLeod

The home team's fine run of form against the Gunners came to a halt when they were narrowly defeated by the odd goal in five. John Barnwell, Johnny MacLeod and Alan Skirton provided the goals which did the damage. Peter Brabrook and Michael Harrison were both on target for the Blues, but their heroics were in vain. Worse still for the west Londoners was their failure to win one of their last eleven league matches. Consequently, no sooner had Tommy Docherty taken on the managerial duties when he and his charges were suffering the shame of 'achieving' Chelsea's first relegation for almost forty years. Finishing in bottom place, and having conceded more goals than anyone else told its own story. Ironically, it would be Arsenal manager George Swindin who would be stepping down at the end of the season after mid-table Arsenal had 'allowed' Tottenham Hotspur and West Ham United to finish above them.

CHELSEA	ARSENAL
1 Bonetti	1 Kelsey
2 Shellito	2 Bacuzzi
3 Butler	3 McCullough
4 Malcolm	4 Clamp
5 Young	5 Brown
6 R Harris	6 Groves
7 Brabrook	7 MacLeod

8 Murray	8 Barnwell
9 Bridges	9 Strong
10 Venables	10 Eastham
11 Harrison	11 Skirton

SEASON 1961-2:
ARSENAL:
Finished 10th; Won 16; Drew 11; Lost 15; Goals for 71; Against 72; Points 43
CHELSEA:
Finished 22nd; Won 9; Drew 10; Lost 23; Goals for 63; Against 94; Points 28

CHELSEA 3 ARSENAL 1; November 16th 1963 (Crowd 47,050) Scorers: Murray Bridges Watson; Eastham

More than eighteen months since their previous encounter and Tommy Docherty's talented youngsters were back with a bang. The second largest league crowd of the season at Stamford Bridge witnessed Billy Wright's team being put to the sword with goals from Barry Bridges, Bert Murray and Ian Watson (who was making only his third of five appearances for the Blues). George Eastham found the target for the away team but his goal was in vain. Better times lay ahead for Eastham when he appeared four days later in England's first floodlit Wembley fixture when Alf Ramsey's team squeezed home 8-3 against Northern Ireland.

CHELSEA	ARSENAL
1 Bonetti	1 Wilson
2 Watson	2 Magill

3 McCreadie	3 McCullough
4 R Harris	4 Brown
5 Mortimore	5 Ure
6 Upton	6 Barnwell
7 Murray	7 MacLeod
8 Tambling	8 Strong
9 Bridges	9 Baker
10 Venables	10 Eastham
11 Blunstone	11 Anderson

ARSENAL 2 CHELSEA 4; March 14th 1964 (Crowd 25,513) Scorers: Neill Baker; Tambling (4)

The home team had no answer to England international Bobby Tambling who emulated Ted Drake (his previous manager) by netting four times in this derby fixture. Joe Baker and Terry Neill each gave the Highbury faithful something to cheer about but this league match will be remembered as the only occasion to date when a Chelsea player scored a hat-trick in a London derby against Arsenal. This impressive triumph for the Blues began a run of seven wins from their last nine league outings which contrasted with a miserable run for the Gunners who won only two of their last eleven league matches. Consequently, the away team was able to finish in a higher position than their north London rivals in addition to defeating them twice in the campaign.

ARSENAL	CHELSEA
1 Furnell	1 Bonetti
2 Bacuzzi	2 Shellito
3 McCullough	3 McCreadie

4 Neill	4 R Harris
5 Ure	5 Mortimore
6 Simpson	6 Upton
7 MacLeod	7 Murray
8 Strong	8 Tambling
9 Baker	9 Bridges
10 Eastham	10 Venables
11 Armstrong	11 Blunstone

SEASON 1963-4:
CHELSEA:
Finished 5th; Won 20; Drew 10; Lost 12; Goals for 72; Against 56; Points 50
ARSENAL:
Finished 8th; Won 17; Drew 11; Lost 14; Goals for 90; Against 82; Points 45

ARSENAL 1 CHELSEA 3; September 26th 1964 (Crowd 54,936) Scorers: Court; Murray Tambling Venables

Highbury's second largest crowd of the season saw the hugely impressive visitors extend their unbeaten start to the league season to ten matches. Prolific scoring duo Bert Murray and Bobby Tambling both found the back of the net while Terry Venables also found the target one month before his own form would merit an international call-up. David Court's goal merely provided the home team with a small crumb of comfort as this first home defeat since March appeared to confirm that Tommy Docherty's exciting team was overtaking the Gunners as London's premier team. The dominance of the 1930s was now a fading memory for the Arsenal faithful.

ARSENAL
1 Furnell
2 Howe
3 Clarke
4 Strong
5 Ferry
6 Neill
7 Skirton
8 Court
9 Baker
10 Eastham
11 Armstrong

CHELSEA
1 Bonetti
2 Shellito
3 McCreadie
4 Hollins
5 Hinton
6 Harris
7 Murray
8 Tambling
9 Bridges
10 Venables
11 Houseman

CHELSEA 2 ARSENAL 1; February 6th 1965 (Crowd 46,798) Scorers: Graham (2); Radford

A double from future Arsenal manager George Graham provided the home team with their first ever back-to-back league doubles against the Gunners. Graham must have clearly left an impression on the Arsenal management, because a year and a half later they signed him! John Radford grabbed a goal for the visitors but there would be no stopping a Chelsea team that were heading for their first top three league finish for ten years. In fact, were it not for a miserable end to the season when the Blues only won one of their last six league matches, a second League Championship would have been achieved.

CHELSEA
1 Bonetti
2 Hinton

ARSENAL
1 Burns
2 Howe

3 McCreadie	3 Clarke
4 Hollins	4 Neill
5 Mortimore	5 Ure
6 Harris	6 Court
7 Murray	7 Skirton
8 Graham	8 Radford
9 Bridges	9 Baker
10 Venables	10 Eastham
11 Tambling	11 Armstrong

SEASON 1964-5:
CHELSEA:
Finished 3rd; Won 24; Drew 8; Lost 10; Goals for 89; Against 54; Points 56
ARSENAL:
Finished 13th; Won 17; Drew 7; Lost 18; Goals for 69; Against 75; Points 41

ARSENAL 1 CHELSEA 3; September 4th 1965 (Crowd 45,456) Scorers: Baker; Graham Bridges Fascione

Highbury's third largest gathering of the season looked on as the Blues cruised to an unprecedented fifth successive league victory. Joe Baker netted for the hosts but his achievement was ruined by the combined goals of England international Barry Bridges, Joe Fascione and George Graham (again). With only one win from their first four league matches, Arsenal appeared set for another disappointing season. Consequently, when the west Londoners paid their next visit to Arsenal, the Gunners would have by then decided that manager Billy Wright was surplus to requirements. For the home following, mid-table positions were intolerable.

ARSENAL	CHELSEA
1 Furnell	1 Bonetti
2 Howe	2 Shellito
3 McCullough	3 McCreadie
4 Neill	4 Hollins
5 Ure	5 Hinton
6 McLintock	6 Harris
7 Sammels	7 Murray
8 Eastham	8 Graham
9 Baker	9 Bridges
10 Court	10 Venables
11 Armstrong	11 Fascione

CHELSEA 0 ARSENAL 0; February 19th 1966 (Crowd 48,641)

The Gunners failed for the sixth successive time to overcome the home team, but at least they restricted them to no goals and a solitary point. It had been more than eight years since both teams last fought out a scoreless draw. Another source of encouragement for the north Londoners was the fact that they brought to an end the best ever run of form by a Chelsea team that had put together no fewer than eight successive league and cup wins. Ironically, the last team that the Blues failed to beat was Arsenal's neighbours Tottenham Hotspur. Nevertheless, for the second successive year Chelsea would finish as London's top team, while Billy Wright's term as Arsenal manager finished with the Gunners uncomfortably close to relegation.

CHELSEA	ARSENAL
1 Bonetti	1 Furnell
2 Harris	2 Howe
3 McCreadie	3 Storey
4 Hollins	4 McLintock
5 Hinton	5 Neill
6 Boyle	6 Ure
7 Bridges	7 Skirton
8 Graham	8 Sammels
9 Osgood	9 Radford
10 Venables	10 Court
11 Tambling (12) Fascione	11 Armstrong

SEASON 1965-6:
CHELSEA:
Finished 5th; Won 22; Drew 7; Lost 13; Goals for 65; Against 53; Points 51
ARSENAL:
Finished 14th; Won 12; Drew 13; Lost 17; Goals for 62; Against 75; Points 37

CHELSEA 3 ARSENAL 1; September 24th 1966 (Crowd 48,001) Scorers: Osgood Tambling (2); Addison

The home team extended their unbeaten run against the visitors to a remarkable seven league matches in front of Stamford Bridge's third largest crowd of the season. The hugely talented Peter Osgood found the back of the net, but he would break a leg eleven days later which would end a promising season for him. Chief architect of the demolition was Bobby Tambling who netted twice, having scored a mere five goals in his last league outing the previous week at Villa Park. Colin Addison gave the away team supporters something to cheer about, but new manager Bertie Mee had now tasted two 3-1 reverses in the same month away to London rivals Tottenham Hotspur and now Chelsea. He would have sufficient opportunities in the next decade to avenge this state of affairs. Meanwhile, both Tommy Baldwin and George Graham both played their last league matches for their respective clubs before they swapped teams.

CHELSEA	ARSENAL
1 Bonetti	1 Furnell
2 Kirkup	2 Simpson
3 McCreadie	3 Storey
4 Hollins	4 McLintock
5 Hinton	5 Ure
6 Harris	6 McGill
7 Boyle	7 Coakley
8 Graham	8 Addison
9 Osgood	9 Baldwin
10 Cooke (12) Thomson	10 Sammels
11 Tambling	11 Walley

ARSENAL 2 CHELSEA 1; February 4th 1967 (Crowd 52,467) Scorers: Graham Armstrong; Tambling

The prolific Bobby Tambling found the back of the Arsenal net again, but the second largest gathering at Highbury in this season saw the Gunners record their first win against the Blues for five years. The two Georges – Armstrong and Graham – were responsible for the result, or at least their

89

goals went a long way towards deciding the outcome. More than 100,000 had witnessed the two league clashes in this season, with both clubs each recording a home triumph. It was a year in which each club had something to be positive about. Arsenal returned to the top half of the league table while Chelsea reached their second FA Cup Final. However, the final was won by Tottenham who also finished third in the league.

ARSENAL	CHELSEA
1 Furnell	1 Bonetti
2 Simpson	2 Thomson
3 Storey	3 McCreadie
4 McLintock	4 Hollins
5 Ure	5 Hinton
6 Neill	6 Harris
7 Neilson	7 Cooke
8 Addison (12) McNab	8 Tambling
9 Graham	9 Hateley
10 Sammels	10 Baldwin
11 Armstrong	11 Houseman

SEASON 1966-7:
ARSENAL:
Finished 7th; Won 16; Drew 14; Lost 12; Goals for 58; Against 47; Points 46
CHELSEA:
Finished 9th; Won 15; Drew 14; Lost 13; Goals for 67; Against 62; Points 44

CHELSEA 2 ARSENAL 1; December 26th 1967 (Crowd 51,672) Scorers: Birchenall (2); Neill (Pen)

In spite of rehabilitating Chelsea Football Club, the charismatic Tommy Docherty was elbowed out in October 1967 after a poor start to the league season. His successor, Dave Sexton, who had been a coach at Arsenal, was entrusted with taking the Blues away from the relegation zone. A pair of goals from recent signing Alan Birchenall helped the home team take another two points on the road to recovery. A successful spot kick from Terry Neill was not sufficient to earn the Gunners a point, but they would have the opportunity in four days time to obtain instant revenge.

CHELSEA
1 Bonetti
2 Kirkup
3 McCreadie
4 Boyle
5 Hinton
6 Harris
7 Cooke
8 Baldwin
9 Osgood
10 Birchenall
11 Tambling

ARSENAL
1 Furnell
2 Storey
3 McNab
4 McLintock
5 Neill
6 Ure
7 Radford
8 Johnston
9 Graham
10 Simpson
11 Armstrong

ARSENAL 1 CHELSEA 1; December 30th 1967 (Crowd 47,157) Scorers: Radford; Osgood (Pen)

Not surprisingly, the Blues were unchanged from their last outing while the home team replaced George Johnston with Jon Sammels. This time, the west Londoners were awarded a penalty kick and Peter Osgood duly obliged. John Radford was on target for the men in red as he and Osgood pressed their claims for an eventual England call-up. Three points from these two back-to-back clashes were evidence that Dave Sexton was guiding his team to safety, and remarkably, by the end of the season, Chelsea had climbed into a top six position, finishing above Arsenal and Tottenham as London's top club, after having looked like relegation candidates.

ARSENAL	CHELSEA
1 Furnell	1 Bonetti
2 Storey	2 Kirkup
3 McNab	3 McCreadie
4 McLintock	4 Boyle
5 Neill	5 Hinton
6 Ure	6 Harris
7 Radford	7 Cooke
8 Sammels	8 Baldwin
9 Graham	9 Osgood
10 Simpson	10 Birchenall
11 Armstrong	11 Tambling

SEASON 1967-8:
CHELSEA:
Finished 6th; Won 18; Drew 12; Lost 12; Goals for 62; Against 68; Points 48
ARSENAL:
Finished 9th; Won 17; Drew 10; Lost 15; Goals for 60; Against 56; Points 44

ARSENAL 0 CHELSEA 1; November 23rd 1968 (Crowd 45,588) Scorer: Houseman

Peter Houseman's first goal of the season secured both points as the Blues condemned the Gunners to their first home defeat since April. In spite of this defeat, the home team had made an excellent start to the league campaign which provided evidence that Bertie Mee was reviving the fortunes of Arsenal. His goalkeeper, Scotsman Bob Wilson, had already obtained no fewer than ten shut-outs from only 23 league and cup matches prior to this contest. The north Londoners were also halfway through a two-legged semi-final duel in the League Cup with Tottenham Hotspur. The away team, having lost three of their last four games, was able to profit from Arsenal's cup distractions.

ARSENAL	CHELSEA
1 Wilson	1 Bonetti
2 Storey	2 Hollins
3 McNab	3 Harris
4 McLintock	4 Osgood
5 Ure	5 Webb
6 Simpson	6 Boyle
7 Radford	7 Baldwin
8 Court	8 Cooke
9 Sammels	9 Birchenall
10 Graham (12) Gould	10 Lloyd
11 Armstrong	11 Houseman

CHELSEA 2 ARSENAL 1; April 14th 1969 (Crowd 38,905) Scorers: Baldwin Webb; Court

The west Londoners finished the season like an express train, recording nine wins from their last thirteen league matches. In their penultimate outing, they succeeded in narrowly overcoming the Gunners for the second time in the campaign. Tommy Baldwin would have taken great pleasure in scoring against a club that had decided he was surplus to requirements. David Webb meanwhile crowned his season with his eighth goal – a commendable total for a defender who actually played in all fifty league and cup matches that Chelsea were engaged in. David Court found the target for the visitors, who in spite of their failings against Chelsea enjoyed a much improved season which culminated in Arsenal finishing as the capital's top team for the first time after 10 lean years. With the Blues perched immediately below them and Tottenham Hotspur in sixth spot it was unusual for three London clubs to be located in the top six. Arsenal would be rewarded with a Fairs Cup place in the following season. Both Arsenal and Chelsea were edging towards glory.

CHELSEA
1 Bonetti
2 Webb
3 Harris
4 Hinton
5 Dempsey
6 Osgood
7 Baldwin
8 Tambling
9 Hutchinson
10 Birchenall
11 Houseman

ARSENAL
1 Wilson
2 Storey
3 McNab
4 McLintock
5 Simpson
6 Graham (12) Neill
7 Robertson
8 Sammels
9 Court
10 Radford
11 Armstrong

SEASON 1968-9:
ARSENAL:
Finished 4th; Won 22; Drew 12; Lost 8; Goals for 56;
Against 27; Points 56
CHELSEA:
Finished 5th; Won 20; Drew 10; Lost 12; Goals for 73;
Against 53; Points 50

CHELSEA 3 ARSENAL 0; September 27th 1969 (Crowd
46,370) Scorers: Baldwin Birchenall (2)

Tommy Baldwin repeated his goalscoring performance of
the same fixture from the spring, while big blond striker
Alan Birchenall emulated his achievement of December
1967 when he scored twice to sink the Gunners at Stamford
Bridge. After an indifferent start to the new campaign, the
Blues knew they could depend on maintaining their Indian
sign over the north Londoners. In fact, this emphatic
triumph was the catalyst for a transformation in Chelsea's
season as they embarked on an eleven games unbeaten
league sequence. By contrast, the away team was in the
midst of a league run that yielded only one narrow win
from twelve attempts. Their unlucky goalkeeper Malcolm
Webster completed his three match league career at Arsenal
on this day as he had begun it – by conceding three goals in
a London derby defeat.

CHELSEA	ARSENAL
1 Bonetti	1 Webster
2 Boyle	2 Storey
3 McCreadie	3 McNab

4 Hollins	4 Court
5 Dempsey	5 McLintock
6 Hinton	6 Simpson
7 Cooke	7 Robertson
8 Houseman	8 Sammels
9 Baldwin	9 Radford
10 Birchenall	10 Graham
11 Osgood	11 George

ARSENAL 0 CHELSEA 3; January 17th 1970 (Crowd 53,793) Scorers: Hollins Baldwin Hutchinson

Dave Sexton's team carried their ascendancy over Arsenal from the 1960s into the new decade which promised so much for his exciting, free-scoring outfit. Tommy Baldwin collected his third goal in consecutive contests against his former employers while Ian Hutchinson also found the target. Also on the scoresheet was John Hollins who had appeared in one international for England in 1967 and who played in all fifty-four league and cup games in this vintage season for Chelsea which climaxed with their captain Ron Harris lifting the FA Cup for the first time in the club's history. The Gunners meanwhile compensated for a disappointing league campaign when their skipper Frank McLintock hoisted aloft the Fairs Cup after a successful conquest of Europe. A new star had started to emerge at Highbury called Ray Kennedy, though he had the misfortune of making his first starting appearance in this 3-0 drubbing. Also, playing in his home debut was recent signing, young Scotsman Peter Marinello who having scored at Old Trafford in his first game had to live up to 'the new George Best' tag that he was labelled with.

Having both won silverware, each team looked forward with relish to the new season.

ARSENAL	CHELSEA
1 Wilson	1 Bonetti
2 Storey	2 Webb
3 McNab	3 McCreadie
4 McLintock	4 Hollins
5 Roberts	5 Dempsey
6 Simpson	6 Harris
7 Marinello	7 Baldwin
8 Sammels	8 Hudson
9 Radford	9 Osgood
10 Kelly (12) George	10 Hutchinson
11 Kennedy	11 Houseman

SEASON 1969-70:
CHELSEA:
Finished 3rd; Won 21; Drew 13; Lost 8; Goals for 70; Against 50; Points 55
ARSENAL:
Finished 12th; Won 12; Drew 18; Lost 12; Goals for 51; Against 49; Points 42

CHELSEA 2 ARSENAL 1; August 29th 1970 (Crowd 53,722) Scorers: Hollins Mulligan; Kelly

Stamford Bridge's second largest league crowd of the season were present to see the FA Cup holders maintain their phenomenal run against the Gunners that had brought only one narrow defeat in their last fifteen matches in this fixture. John Hollins and Paddy Mulligan scored the goals which extended Chelsea's unbeaten start to the league campaign to five games. Eddie Kelly found the net for Arsenal, but it was not enough to prevent the north Londoners' first league defeat of the new term. With the Blues overtaking the men in red after this result, the omens were pointing misleadingly to another season in which Chelsea would outshine Arsenal.

CHELSEA	ARSENAL
1 Bonetti	1 Wilson
2 Mulligan	2 Rice
3 Harris	3 McNab
4 Hollins	4 Kelly
5 Dempsey	5 McLintock
6 Hinton	6 Roberts
7 Weller	7 Armstrong
8 Hudson	8 Storey
9 Osgood	9 Nelson
10 Hutchinson (12) Cooke	10 Kennedy
11 Houseman	11 Graham

ARSENAL 2 CHELSEA 0; April 3rd 1971 (Crowd 62,087)
Scorer: Kennedy (2)

Arsenal's largest home crowd for more than two years witnessed young Ray Kennedy grab a double which helped the Gunners collect two more precious points en route to a possible League Championship. Kennedy's impact in this historic season is clearly demonstrated by the fact that he would finish with nineteen league goals which put him third equal in the First Division goalscoring charts. Meanwhile,

Bob Wilson was collecting his 27th clean sheet out of a season's total of thirty-seven. Playing in front of him George Armstrong shared Wilson's distinction of playing in all 64 games, while John Radford, Pat Rice, Frank McLintock as well as Ray Kennedy appeared in sixty-three games, and England internationals Bob McNab and Peter Storey contributed in a mere sixty-two domestic games. This amazing roll-call goes a long way towards explaining why Bertie Mee's team emerged from almost nowhere to grab a phenomenal league and cup double. This victory was in fact one of nine straight wins for the north Londoners in the league, with Bob Wilson achieving the fourth of five successive league shut-outs. Consequently, the men in red appeared as if by magic to 'steal' the League Championship away from their rivals Leeds United, who were bridesmaids for the second successive year. Arsenal's cause had been helped by the Blues who had defeated Don Revie's team 3-1 the previous weekend. The away team, for their part, won only three times in their last ten league matches to slip out of the top three and be overtaken by amongst others League Cup winners Tottenham Hotspur. In mitigation, the west Londoners were somewhat distracted by a European adventure which saw them lift the Cup Winners' Cup after defeating the mighty Real Madrid 2-1 in the final. All in all, it was a vintage year for Chelsea and especially Arsenal with London's big three clubs sharing four pieces of silverware between them.

ARSENAL
1 Wilson
2 Rice
3 McNab

CHELSEA
1 Phillips
2 Harris
3 McCreadie

4 Storey	4 Hollins
5 McLintock	5 Dempsey
6 Simpson	6 Webb
7 Armstrong (12) Kelly	7 Baldwin
8 Graham	8 Hudson
9 Radford	9 Osgood
10 Kennedy	10 Cooke
11 George	11 Houseman

SEASON 1970-1:
ARSENAL:
Finished 1st; Won 29; Drew 7; Lost 6; Goals for 71; Against 29; Points 65
CHELSEA:
Finished 6th; Won 18; Drew 15; Lost 9; Goals for 52; Against 42; Points 51

ARSENAL 3 CHELSEA 0; August 14th 1971 (Crowd 49,174) Scorers: McLintock Kennedy Radford

England's reigning league and FA Cup champions kicked off their new season in the best possible way – courtesy of goals from Ray Kennedy, Frank McLintock and England centre-forward John Radford. After having spent a decade in the doldrums, the home team suddenly could do no wrong. Two convincing wins in 1971 against Chelsea was extra evidence of Arsenal's revival. After all, the Gunners had until this year appeared rather clueless at how to cope with the west Londoners. In spite of this setback, Dave Sexton's team seemed well equipped to challenge alongside Arsenal for further honours.

ARSENAL	CHELSEA
1 Wilson	1 Bonetti
2 Rice	2 McCreadie
3 McNab	3 Harris
4 Storey	4 Hollins
5 McLintock	5 Dempsey
6 Simpson	6 Webb
7 Armstrong	7 Smethurst
8 Kelly	8 Hudson
9 Radford	9 Osgood
10 Kennedy	10 Baldwin
11 Graham	11 Houseman

CHELSEA 1 ARSENAL 2; October 16th 1971 (Crowd 52,338) Scorers: Osgood: Kennedy (2)

Barely six months after netting twice to sink Chelsea, Ray Kennedy recorded another derby double to nail down Arsenal's first triumph at Stamford Bridge since 1962. Kennedy would soon earn the distinction of having scored in five successive derby games against both Chelsea and Tottenham Hotspur between April and November 1971. The Gunners had now amassed a run of six wins from their last seven league matches, which gave rise to hopes of retaining their league trophy, but three consecutive defeats in November and again in March 1972 ruined their chances. Peter Osgood found the target for the Blues, but like the men in red, the west Londoners would suffer a Wembley cup final setback in 1972. Two defeats in their last two league matches also enabled Tottenham Hotspur to squeeze between Arsenal and Chelsea in the league.

CHELSEA	ARSENAL
1 Bonetti	1 Wilson
2 Boyle	2 Rice
3 Harris	3 Nelson
4 Hollins	4 McLintock
5 Webb	5 Roberts
6 Hinton	6 George
7 Hudson	7 Armstrong
8 Baldwin	8 Kelly (12) Simpson
9 Osgood	9 Radford
10 Kember	10 Kennedy
11 Cooke	11 Graham

SEASON 1971-2:
ARSENAL:
Finished 5th; Won 22; Drew 8; Lost 12; Goals for 58; Against 40; Points 52
CHELSEA:
Finished 7th; Won 18; Drew 12; Lost 12; Goals for 58; Against 49; Points 48

ARSENAL 1 CHELSEA 1; September 2nd 1972 (Crowd 46,675) Scorers: Webb (OG); Cooke

Goal provider Charlie Cooke turned into a goalscorer as he ensured that the home team would drop their first point at Highbury in this new league season. However, the Gunners were grateful to David Webb who put the ball through his own net, thereby extending Arsenal's highly promising start to seven league matches unbeaten.

ARSENAL   CHELSEA

1 Barnett	1 Bonetti
2 Rice	2 Mulligan
3 McNab	3 McCreadie
4 Storey	4 Hollins
5 McLintock	5 Webb
6 Simpson	6 Harris
7 Armstrong (12) George	7 Garland
8 Ball	8 Kember (12) Droy
9 Radford	9 Osgood
10 Kennedy	10 Houseman
11 Graham	11 Cooke

CHELSEA 0 ARSENAL 1; January 20th 1973 (Crowd 36,292) Scorer: Kennedy

Like Cliff Bastin, Freddie Cox and Ted Drake before him, Ray Kennedy had clearly acquired a taste for scoring goals against Chelsea. Having narrowly overcome Leicester City 2-1 at Filbert Street a few days earlier in an FA Cup third round replay, the Gunners were now in the midst of an impressive fifteen games unbeaten league and cup sequence which hinted at the very real possibility of more silverware at the end of the season. However, only one win from their last six league matches put paid to Arsenal's league hopes, allowing Liverpool to pip Arsenal to the League Championship post. Meanwhile, in the FA Cup, the north Londoners' ambitions would be severely tested when they and cup specialists Chelsea were drawn together for a reunion in the sixth round of England's premier cup competition.

CHELSEA   ARSENAL

1 Phillips	1 Wilson
2 Locke	2 Rice
3 Harris	3 McNab
4 Hollins	4 Storey
5 Dempsey	5 Blockley
6 Webb	6 Simpson
7 Baldwin	7 Armstrong
8 Hudson	8 Ball
9 Osgood	9 Radford
10 Kember	10 Kennedy
11 Garner	11.Kelly(12) McLintock

CHELSEA 2 ARSENAL 2; March 17th 1973 (Crowd 37,685) FA Cup 6th Round Scorers: Osgood Hollins; Ball George

It had been 21 years since both clubs had engaged each other in an FA Cup battle when Arsenal of course won a semi-final replay 3-0. On this occasion, both combatants shared four goals, with Alan Ball and Charlie George netting goals for the visitors while England internationals John Hollins and Peter Osgood found the back of the net for the Blues. With this Saint Patrick's Day encounter finishing deadlocked, a replay at Highbury would be required to separate the two London rivals.

CHELSEA	ARSENAL
1 Phillips	1 Wilson
2 Locke	2 Rice
3 McCreadie	3 McNab
4 Hollins	4 Storey
5 Dempsey	5 McLintock

6 Hinton	6 Simpson
7 Garland	7 Armstrong
8 Hudson	8 Ball
9 Osgood	9 George
10 Kember	10 Kennedy
11 Houseman	11 Kelly

ARSENAL 2 CHELSEA 1; March 20th 1973 (Crowd 62,746) FA Cup 6th Round Replay Scorers: Ball (Pen) Kennedy; Houseman

England World Cup hero Alan Ball scored from the spot while Ray Kennedy was on hand to inflict more pain on the away team. Chelsea's FA Cup Final hero Peter Houseman found the target for the Blues, but his effort could not prevent the Gunners from progressing to the last four of the FA Cup for the third consecutive year. Four years later Houseman would meet a premature end when he and his wife Sally were both killed in a car crash. Meanwhile, the west Londoners slipped out of the top ten for the first season in ten years. Chelsea's golden era can be said to have ended with this narrow cup defeat in front of Arsenal's highest ever attendance figure for a Chelsea visit. The hosts were expected to reach Wembley on the back of this triumph, but instead succumbed surprisingly to the eventual winners Sunderland from the Second Division.

ARSENAL	CHELSEA
1 Wilson	1 Phillips
2 Rice	2 Hollins
3 McNab	3 McCreadie
4 Storey	4 Kember

5 McLintock	5 Dempsey
6 Simpson	6 Hinton
7 Armstrong	7 Garland
8 Ball	8 Hudson
9 George	9 Osgood
10 Kennedy	10 Garner
11 Kelly	11 Houseman

SEASON 1972-3:
ARSENAL:
Finished 2nd; Won 23; Drew 11; Lost 8; Goals for 57; Against 43; Points 57
CHELSEA:
Finished 12th; Won 13; Drew 14; Lost 15; Goals for 49; Against 51; Points 40

ARSENAL 0 CHELSEA 0; November 17th 1973 (Crowd 38,677)

A clean sheet from England international Peter Bonetti helped the visitors to a sharing of the points in what would prove to be Dave Sexton's last appearance at Highbury as Chelsea manager. Bonetti's opposite number, Scotland international goalkeeper Bob Wilson also achieved a shut-out as these two goal-shy teams were in the process of slipping down the charts of English football. Chelsea had now failed for the eighth successive time to defeat Arsenal.

ARSENAL	CHELSEA
1 Wilson	1 Bonetti
2 Rice	2 Locke
3 McNab	3 Hollins

4 Storey	4 Kember
5 Simpson	5 Webb
6 Kelly	6 Harris
7 Ball	7 Garland
8 George	8 Britton
9 Hornsby	9 Osgood
10 Kennedy	10 Baldwin
11 Armstrong	11 Houseman

CHELSEA 1 ARSENAL 3; April 13th 1974 (Crowd 29,152) Scorers: Swain; Kennedy (2) Radford

It was a measure of the decay at both clubs that this fixture should attract less than thirty thousand spectators for the first time in just over ten years. Having been giants in English football at the start of the 1970s, both Arsenal and especially Chelsea had become also-rans by the middle of the decade. Nevertheless, the north Londoners still had cause to celebrate as another double from Ray Kennedy as well as a goal from John Radford ensured that the men in red would collect their first maximum points away from home since a derby encounter at Upton Park the previous November. Meanwhile, Kenny Swain's first goal for the Blues was the only one they managed to record in their last five league matches as the season ended in a miserable manner.

CHELSEA	ARSENAL
1 Phillips	1 Wilson
2 Harris	2 Rice
3 Sparrow	3 Nelson

4 Hollins	4 Storey
5 Droy	5 Blockley
6 Hinton	6 Kelly (12) Simpson
7 Swain	7 Armstrong
8 R Wilkins	8 Ball
9 Houseman	9 Radford
10 Garner	10 Kennedy
11 Cooke (12) Hutchinson	11 George

SEASON 1973-4:
ARSENAL:
Finished 10th; Won 14; Drew 14; Lost 14; Goals for 49; Against 51; Points 42
CHELSEA:
Finished 17th; Won 12; Drew 13; Lost 17; Goals for 56; Against 60; Points 37

CHELSEA 0 ARSENAL 0; September 14th 1974 (Crowd 34,596)

The omens for the season ahead were already plain to see. The away team failed for the fourth time to score a goal from their first seven league matches, four of which they had already lost. The Blues meanwhile had failed to find the back of the net for the third time from four home league matches, but they could console themselves that their predicament was not apparently as desperate as Arsenal's, as the visitors were in the midst of a wretched twelve games without a win sequence. At least Jimmy Rimmer of Arsenal and Chelsea's Welsh international goalkeeper John Phillips could hold their heads up high on account of the clean sheets that they and their defences had obtained on this day.

For all of Arsenal's troubles, it would be Dave Sexton and not Bertie Mee who would be walking through the exit door a month later.

CHELSEA	ARSENAL
1 Phillips	1 Rimmer
2 Locke	2 Kelly
3 Houseman	3 Simpson
4 Hollins	4 Storey
5 Dempsey	5 Blockley
6 Harris	6 Matthews
7 Hay	7 Armstrong
8 Garland	8 George
9 Cooke	9 Radford
10 Hutchinson	10 Kidd
11 Sissons	11 Brady

ARSENAL 1 CHELSEA 2; December 26th 1974 (Crowd 33,784) Scorers: Ball (Pen); Garland (2)

For the second successive year Alan Ball was able to punish the Blues with a successful spot kick at Highbury. Nevertheless, the away team remained (for the time being) above the Gunners, due to a double from Chris Garland, which secured Chelsea's first win over the north Londoners since the heady days of August 1970. With three wins and a draw from their first four league matches from December, the west Londoners, now under the stewardship of Ron Suart, seemed in less peril than the men in red. However, while Arsenal staggered to eventual safety, it was Chelsea who went in to free-fall on the back of only three wins in their remaining nineteen league engagements. Consequently, Ron Suart was replaced by Chelsea favourite

Eddie McCreadie the following spring as the Blues bowed out of Division One, having scored fewer goals than any other team in the top flight. Of the five London teams in the First Division, none finished in the top ten, with Arsenal and Tottenham each narrowly avoiding relegation.

ARSENAL	CHELSEA
1 Rimmer	1 Phillips
2 Rice	2 Locke
3 McNab	3 Harris
4 Kelly	4 Hollins
5 Mancini	5 Droy
6 Simpson	6 Hay
7 Storey	7 Cooke
8 Ball	8 R Wilkins
9 Radford	9 Garland
10 Kidd	10 Hutchinson
11 Cropley	11 Houseman

SEASON 1974-5:
ARSENAL:
Finished 16th; Won 13; Drew 11; Lost 18; Goals for 47; Against 49; Points 37
CHELSEA:
Finished 21st; Won 9; Drew 15; Lost 18; Goals for 42; Against 72; Points 33

ARSENAL 2 CHELSEA 1; October 26th 1976 (Crowd 52,305) League Cup 4th Round Scorers: Ross Stapleton; Hay

Having been thumped 5-1 and 4-1 in their last two league matches, Arsenal bounced back with a narrow triumph in their first ever League Cup encounter with the Blues. Although ex-Glasgow Celtic star David Hay's goal was unable to earn a replay, the visitors could take comfort from a highly promising start to their league campaign which seemed to suggest that their exile to Division Two would be a brief one. New Arsenal manager Terry Neill had goals from Trevor Ross and Frank Stapleton to thank for this cup victory over his old sparring partner, ex Chelsea full-back Eddie McCreadie. Highbury's largest crowd for more than eighteen months witnessed this cup clash.

ARSENAL	CHELSEA
1 Rimmer	1 Phillips
2 Rice	2 Locke
3 Nelson	3 G Wilkins
4 Ross	4 Stanley
5 Simpson	5 Wicks
6 Howard	6 Hay
7 Ball	7 Bason (12) Harris
8 Brady	8 R Wilkins
9 Macdonald	9 Finnieston
10 Stapleton	10 Lewington
11 Armstrong	11 Swain

ARSENAL 3 CHELSEA 0; December 26th 1977 (Crowd 46,074) Scorers: Price Rix O'Leary

It was three years to the day since both clubs had been involved in a league exchange, and the Gunners took the opportunity to avenge Chelsea's successful visit to Highbury on Boxing Day 1974. This time, newly-promoted Chelsea had no answer to goals from David Price, Graham

Rix and David O'Leary who thumped home the third goal. Under new manager Ken Shellito, the Blues were finding life in the fast lane to be beyond their abilities. The Gunners meanwhile were enjoying a revival under Terry Neill, who had drastically altered Arsenal's playing personnel. This visit of the west Londoners presented Highbury with its second largest league gathering of the season

ARSENAL	CHELSEA
1 Jennings	1 Bonetti
2 Rice	2 Harris
3 Nelson	3 Sparrow
4 Price	4 Britton
5 O'Leary	5 Droy
6 Young	6 Wicks
7 Brady	7 Aylott (12) Lewington
8 Sunderland	8 R Wilkins
9 Macdonald	9 Langley
10 Stapleton (12) Simpson	10 Swain
11 Rix	11 Walker

CHELSEA 0 ARSENAL 0; March 27th 1978 (Crowd 40,764)

Stamford Bridge's second highest league crowd of this campaign were present to witness the home team defy all expectations by earning a clean sheet, after failing to do so in their previous seventeen league matches. Former England goalkeeper Peter Bonetti had stooped to pick the ball out of the back of his net numerous times against the Arsenal, but with the help of his defence he collected his seventh and final shutout against his formidable foes. Meanwhile, Pat Jennings and his defence helped themselves to a pair of clean sheets against a Chelsea team who struggled to cope with life back in the elite, yet they finished as one of London's top two teams in the top flight for the first time since the turn of the decade. Nevertheless, a shocking start to the following season meant that this would be Ken Shellito's last appointment with Arsenal as Chelsea manager. As for Arsenal, a failure to score in three of their last four games cost them a top three place as well as condemning them to a narrow defeat in the FA Cup Final.

CHELSEA	ARSENAL
1 Bonetti	1 Jennings
2 Locke	2 Rice
3 Harris	3 Nelson
4 Britton	4 Price
5 Droy	5 O'Leary
6 Wicks	6 Young
7 Finnieston	7 Brady
8 Swain	8 Rix
9 Langley	9 Macdonald
10 Lewington	10 Stapleton
11 Hay	11 Hudson

SEASON 1977-8:
ARSENAL:
Finished 5th; Won 21; Drew 10; Lost 11; Goals for 60; Against 37; Points 52
CHELSEA:
Finished 16th; Won 11; Drew 14; Lost 17; Goals for 46; Against 69; Points 36

ARSENAL 5 CHELSEA 2; April 16th 1979 (Crowd 37,232) Scorers: Stapleton (2) O'Leary Sunderland Price; Langley Walker

More than twelve months passed before the next instalment of Arsenal and Chelsea's local dispute. It was an occasion well worth waiting for – as far as the home supporters were concerned. Prolific striker Frank Stapleton added two more goals towards a league total of seventeen which was the fourth highest in the First Division. Fellow Republic of Ireland international David O'Leary repeated his goalscoring effort from Chelsea's last visit to Highbury. David Price also greeted Chelsea's visit with another goal as he had done on Boxing Day 1977. Alan Sunderland also got on the goals bandwagon as his team achieved their first five goals haul against the west Londoners since March 1958. Goals from Tommy Langley and Clive Walker were but a footnote on Arsenal's emphatic triumph. Victory for Arsenal was all the more-sweeter as Chelsea's new supremo was Terry Neill's compatriot, former Spurs maestro Danny Blanchflower. It also came as no surprise that Chelsea would finish a wretched season by conceding far more goals than any other team in Division One. Six days earlier Frank Stapleton had also secured a league double triumph over Tottenham Hotspur, but after this mauling, Arsenal failed to win any of their last five league matches as they became distracted by an urgent appointment with Manchester United in the FA Cup Final.

ARSENAL
1 Jennings

CHELSEA
1 Borota

2 Rice	2 G Wilkins
3 Nelson	3 Stride
4 Talbot	4 Bannon
5 O'Leary	5 Droy
6 Walford	6 Sitton
7 Brady	7 Fillery
8 Sunderland	8 R Wilkins
9 Stapleton	9 Aylott (12) Walker
10 Price	10 Langley
11 Rix	11 Stanley

CHELSEA 1 ARSENAL 1; May 14th 1979 (Crowd 30,705) Scorers: Stanley; Macdonald

Forty-eight hours after an unforgettable 3-2 Wembley triumph in the FA Cup Final, Terry Neill generously presented the legendary 'Supermac' Malcolm Macdonald with his first game since August. While young Paul Vaessen made his Arsenal debut, Macdonald marked the occasion by scoring in what would be his last ever competitive game. Gary Stanley scored against the FA Cup winners, but his team had long since been relegated to Division Two after a thoroughly depressing season for Chelsea. Both Stanley and his goal-keeper Peter Bonetti finished their careers with the Blues after this derby encounter. Peter Bonetti had played 729 major games for Chelsea.

CHELSEA	ARSENAL
1 Bonetti	1 Jennings
2 Chivers	2 Rice
3 Harris	3 Nelson

4 Bannon	4 Talbot
5 Droy	5 O'Leary
6 Sitton	6 Young
7 Stanley	7 Brady
8 Aylott	8 Vaessen
9 Osgood	9 Macdonald
10 Langley	10 Devine
11 Walker	11 Rix

SEASON 1978-9:
ARSENAL:
Finished 7th; Won 17; Drew 14; Lost 11; Goals for 61; Against 48; Points 48
CHELSEA:
Finished 22nd; Won 5; Drew 10; Lost 27; Goals for 44; Against 92; Points 20

ARSENAL 1 CHELSEA 1; August 25th 1984 (45,329)
Scorers: Mariner; Dixon

After an unenviable five year spell in Division Two, the mercurial visitors returned to Highbury to achieve a commendable draw. The Second Division champions had England hopeful Kerry Dixon to thank for earning John Neal's team a point. England international striker Paul Mariner was on target for Don Howe's outfit, which featured recent signing Viv Anderson for his first league outing with the Gunners. Ex-Aberdeen central defender Doug Rougvie also made his first league appearance for newly-promoted Chelsea.

ARSENAL   CHELSEA

1 Jennings	1 Niedzwieckie
2 Anderson	2 Lee
3 Sansom	3 Rougvie
4 Talbot	4 Pates
5 O'Leary	5 McLaughlin
6 Caton	6 Jasper
7 Robson	7 Nevin
8 Davis	8 Spackman
9 Mariner	9 Dixon
10 Woodcock	10 Speedie
11 Allinson	11 Canoville

CHELSEA 1 ARSENAL 1; January 19th 1985 (Crowd 34,752) Scorers: Speedie; Mariner

Both clubs shared two goals and two points again – with Paul Mariner helping himself to another goal while Scotsman David Speedie found the back of the net for the Blues. Steve Williams made his first starting appearance for the away team, who will not have fond memories of January 1985, having lost at home to Tottenham Hotspur on New Year's Day and then going on to suffer a humiliating 1-0 FA Cup Fourth Round exit at the hands of York City. The west Londoners eventually overtook Arsenal to finish as London's second top team for the first time since 1978. Nevertheless, John Neal moved 'upstairs' in the close season to make way for Chelsea favourite and ex-Arsenal player John Hollins.

CHELSEA	ARSENAL
1 Niedzwieckie	1 Lukic
2 Wood	2 Anderson

3 Rougvie
4 Pates
5 McLaughlin
6 Jones
7 Nevin (12) Lee
8 Spackman
9 Dixon
10 Speedie
11 Canoville

3 Sansom
4 Talbot
5 O'Leary
6 Caton
7 Robson
8 Williams
9 Mariner
10 Woodcock
11 C Nicholas

SEASON 1984-5:
CHELSEA:
Finished 6th; Won 18; Drew 12; Lost 12; Goals for 63; Against 48; Points 66
ARSENAL:
Finished 7th; Won 19; Drew 9; Lost 14; Goals for 61; Against 49; Points 66

CHELSEA 2 ARSENAL 1; September 21st 1985 (Crowd 33,241) Scorers: Nevin Spackman (Pen); Nicholas

Goals from Pat Nevin and Nigel Spackman (from the penalty spot) presented the home team with their first triumph against Arsenal since a similar score was achieved at Highbury as far back as December 1974. It was a particularly special occasion for both Kevin McAllister who was making his first start for the Blues and ex-Tottenham player Mickey Hazard who was playing in his Chelsea debut. With five wins and three draws from their first nine league outings, the west Londoners had made their best start to a league campaign since 1966. Not only did the west Londoners overtake the Gunners with this victory, but they appeared to be hinting at a possible challenge for the championship. Former Glasgow Celtic favourite Charlie Nicholas found the target for Arsenal, but his team left Stamford Bridge empty-handed.

CHELSEA	ARSENAL
1 Niedzwieckie	1 Lukic
2 Wood	2 Anderson
3 Rougvie	3 Sansom
4 Isaac	4 Davis
5 McLaughlin	5 O'Leary
6 Bumstead	6 Caton
7 Nevin	7 Robson
8 Hazard(12)Spackman	8 Allinson
9 Dixon	9 Nicholas
10 McAllister	10 Woodcock
11 Canoville	11 Rix

ARSENAL 2 CHELSEA 0; April 29th 1986 (Crowd 24,025) Scorers: Anderson Nicholas

Viv Anderson and Charlie Nicholas scored the goals which provided the hosts with their first win over Chelsea since April 1979. Having looked like championship contenders at one stage, the away team ran out of steam and finished a highly promising campaign with four successive defeats. Nevertheless, they still had the consolation of finishing narrowly above Arsenal for the second consecutive season. The Gunners' victory in this contest had ended a miserable run for them that yielded only one win from eight games. At the end of the season Don Howe would hand the managerial baton on to former Arsenal and Chelsea favourite George Graham. As the curtains began to fall on another league campaign, this encounter represented one of the last chances for players in each team to push for a place in the England and Scotland World Cup squads that would soon depart for the finals in Mexico. With neither club chasing major honours, this derby was played out in front of the lowest crowd for such a fixture since December 1956.

ARSENAL	CHELSEA
1 Lukic	1 Godden
2 Anderson	2 Wood
3 Sansom	3 Rougvie
4 Keown	4 Pates (12) Jones
5 O'Leary	5 McLaughlin
6 Adams	6 Bumstead
7 Robson	7 Nevin
8 Davis	8 Spackman
9 Nicholas	9 Dixon
10 Woodcock	10 Speedie
11 Rix (12) Quinn	11 Murphy

SEASON 1985-6:
CHELSEA:
Finished 6th; Won 20; Drew 11; Lost 11; Goals for 57; Against 56; Points 71
ARSENAL:
Finished 7th; Won 20; Drew 9; Lost 13; Goals for 49; Against 47; Points 69

ARSENAL 3 CHELSEA 1; October 25th 1986 (Crowd 32,990) Scorers: Rocastle Hayes (2); Bumstead

Arsenal's second win of this year over the visitors was at least played out in front of a larger crowd than the previous one back in the spring. As he had done in their last home league match, Martin Hayes slotted home a penalty, as part of a double, while future Chelsea player David Rocastle recorded his first goal of the season. Although the dependable John Bumstead found the back of the net for the away team, the west Londoners were already slipping back into mediocrity after three encouraging seasons. Meanwhile, George Graham was beginning to work his magic at Highbury as this was the home team's fourth successive league win in a spell that would extend to twenty-two games unbeaten.

ARSENAL	CHELSEA
1 Lukic	1 Godden
2 Anderson	2 Wood
3 Sansom	3 Rougvie
4 Williams	4 Pates (12) Lee
5 O'Leary	5 McLaughlin
6 Adams	6 Bumstead
7 Rocastle	7 Nevin
8 Davis	8 Jones
9 Quinn (12) Allinson	9 Dixon
10 Groves	10 McAllister
11 Hayes	11 Murphy

CHELSEA 1 ARSENAL 0; March 7th 1987 (Crowd 29,301) Scorer: West

The men in red were en route to their highest league finish for six years, but on this day they succumbed to a narrow defeat when nineteen year old Colin West scored inside the first five minutes of his debut. West could never match the high expectations that this remarkable start thrust upon his subsequent career. Also making his first appearance for the home team was eighteen year old Scottish substitute Billy Dodds who would go on to terrorise defences and goalkeepers north of the border. After looking like relegation candidates at Christmas, the Blues had staged a commendable recovery that produced nine wins (including this one) in thirteen league matches. Arsenal was still perhaps cock-a-hoop, having narrowly overcome their neighbours Tottenham Hotspur in a League Cup Semi-Final replay three days earlier. The Gunners remarkably were in the midst of a wretched league spell that yielded no wins and only two goals from ten outings. Although their league title ambitions were going up in smoke, George Graham's team held their nerve to lift the League Cup in April.

CHELSEA	ARSENAL
1 Godden	1 Lukic
2 Clark	2 Anderson
3 Dublin	3 Sansom
4 Pates	4 Thomas
5 McLaughlin	5 O'Leary
6 Wood	6 Adams
7 Nevin	7 Rocastle
8 Jones	8 Caeser
9 Lee (12) Dodds	9 Quinn
10 West	10 Allinson
11 Wegerle	11 Hayes (12) Merson

SEASON 1986-7:
ARSENAL:
Finished 4th; Won 20; Drew 10; Lost 12; Goals for 58; Against 35; Points 70
CHELSEA:
Finished 14th; Won 13; Drew 13; Lost 16; Goals for 53; Against 64; Points 52

ARSENAL 3 CHELSEA 1; November 3rd 1987 (Crowd 40,230) Scorers: Richardson (2) Wegerle (OG); Nevin

Revitalised Arsenal notched up their twelfth win in a great sequence of fourteen straight wins in league and cup. Kevin Richardson netted twice and Roy Wegerle (later to become a professional golfer) presented the Gunners with an own goal, not that they needed any generous gestures from the Blues. Pat Nevin helped himself to a goal, but the visitors had to adjust to life without goal-keeper Eddie Niedzwieckie whose career was ended the previous week by an injury. Regrettably for the west Londoners this defeat began a dreadful run which yielded only one narrow win against Derby County in their remaining 26 league matches. Consequently, when the Gunners next visited Stamford Bridge, John Hollins had been sacked.

ARSENAL	CHELSEA
1 Lukic	1 Freestone
2 Thomas	2 Clark
3 Sansom	3 Dorigo
4 Williams	4 Pates
5 O'Leary	5 McLaughlin

6 Adams	6 Wood
7 Rocastle	7 Nevin
8 Davis	8 Wegerle (12) K Wilson
9 Smith	9 Coady
10 Groves	10 Durie
11 Richardson	11 C. Wilson

CHELSEA 1 ARSENAL 1; April 2nd 1988 (Crowd 26,084) Scorers: Hazard; McLaughlin (OG)

Bobby Campbell was now the home team's acting manager as the Blues were desperately attempting to steer clear of the relegation abyss. Mickey Hazard found the target as the hosts earned themselves a draw which in most circumstances would be deemed a commendable result. However, with only five league matches remaining, a home win was desperately required if Chelsea were to avoid the dreaded promotion/relegation play-offs. Meanwhile big Joe McLaughlin's own goal enabled the men in red to extend their unbeaten run in the league to seven games. Like Chelsea, Arsenal were now drawing too many matches, having secured their fourth consecutive league draw, while the west Londoners had now drawn five of their last six games. It would be a spring of woe as Arsenal suffered defeat in the League Cup Final to Luton Town, but this disappointment hardly compares with Chelsea's exit to the Second Division via play-offs and hooligan trouble.

CHELSEA	ARSENAL
1 Hitchcock	1 Lukic
2 Clarke	2 Dixon

3 Dorigo	3 Winterburn
4 Wicks	4 Williams
5 McLaughlin	5 Caesar
6 Wood	6 Adams
7 Nevin	7 Rocastle
8 Hazard	8 Davis
9 Dixon (14) West	9 Quinn
10 Durie (12) Hall	10 Groves
11 Bumstead	11 Hayes

SEASON 1987-8:
ARSENAL:
Finished 6th; Won 18; Drew 12; Lost 10; Goals for 58; Against 39; Points 66
CHELSEA:
Finished 18th; Won 9; Drew 15; Lost 16; Goals for 50; Against 68; Points 42

CHELSEA 0 ARSENAL 0; September 30th 1989 (Crowd 31,833)

The futility of Chelsea's relegation in the spring of 1988 was clearly demonstrated when roughly the same team emphatically stormed to the Second Division Championship. On this day, Bobby Campbell's newly-promoted side held their own against the new First Division champions. Stamford Bridge's largest crowd since the fateful play-off final in May 1988 witnessed this stalemate. John Lukic and his defence were now collecting their sixth clean sheet from only eight outings since the Charity Shield, while Dave Beasant and his defence were recording their fourth shutout from the first eight league matches. With only one defeat from their first eight league outings, each team was proving to be difficult to score against and to overcome.

CHELSEA	ARSENAL
1 Beasant	1 Lukic
2 Clarke	2 Dixon
3 Dorigo	3 Winterburn
4 Roberts (12) Bumstead	4 Thomas
5 Lee	5 O'Leary
6 Monkou	6 Adams
7 Dickens	7 Rocastle (12) Merson
8 Nicholas	8 Richardson
9 Dixon	9 Smith
10 K Wilson	10 Groves
11 Hazard	11 Hayes

ARSENAL 0 CHELSEA 1; March 17th 1990 (Crowd 33,805) Scorer: Bumstead

With five defeats from their previous ten league matches, it was becoming apparent that the Gunners would not make a successful defence of their hard-fought championship title. Not only would the north Londoners fail to lift any major trophies in this disappointing season but they failed to beat or even score against Chelsea. Dave Beasant became only the second Blues goalkeeper (after Peter Bonetti in 1969/70) to keep two clean sheets in a season against the men in red. On the seventeenth anniversary of a famous 2-2 cup encounter at Stamford Bridge between the two London rivals, a goal from John Bumstead created its own piece of 'history.' To be precise, Bumstead's winning effort provided the west Londoners with their last league win at Highbury in the twentieth century. Ex-Arsenal midfielder Peter Nicholas was part of the winning team. While Arsenal were frustrated with finishing fourth in the league, Chelsea were encouraged by their fifth place, immediately below Tottenham and Arsenal, their highest finish since 1970.

ARSENAL	CHELSEA
1 Lukic	1 Beasant
2 Dixon	2 Hall
3 Winterburn	3 Dorigo
4 Thomas	4 Bumstead
5 Bould	5 Johnsen
6 Adams	6 Monkou
7 Rocastle (12) Hayes	7 McAllister
8 Richardson	8 Nicholas
9 Smith	9 Dixon
10 Campbell (14) O'Leary	10 Durie
11 Groves	11 K. Wilson

SEASON 1989-90:
ARSENAL:
Finished 4th; Won 18; Drew 8; Lost 12; Goals for 54; Against 38; Points 62
CHELSEA:
Finished 5th; Won 16; Drew 12; Lost 10; Goals for 58; Against 50; Points 60

ARSENAL 4 CHELSEA 1; September 15th 1990 (Crowd 41,516) Scorers: Limpar Dixon (Pen) Merson Rocastle; Wilson

After both clubs had finished next to one another in the previous campaign, the gulf in class suddenly widened after Arsenal's most emphatic triumph against Chelsea since 1979. Kevin Wilson's goal had no impact on the eventual result, as the home team swept to a storming victory, courtesy of goals from English trio Lee Dixon (from the penalty spot), Paul Merson and David Rocastle, as well as a goal from flying Swede Anders Limpar. The away team was in the midst of a poor start to the new season that only produced two narrow wins from their first ten league matches. By contrast, this resounding win extended Arsenal's unbeaten start to five games. Andy Linighan, who came on as a substitute, made his first appearance for the home team in this one-sided contest.

ARSENAL
1 Seaman
2 Dixon
3 Winterburn
4 Thomas
5 Bould (14) Linighan
6 Adams
7 Rocastle
8 Davis
9 Groves (12) Campbell
10 Merson
11 Limpar

CHELSEA
1 Beasant
2 Hall
3 Dorigo
4 Monkou
5 Cundy
6 Lee
7 Townsend
8 Nicholas (12) McAllister
9 Dixon
10 Wilson
11 Bumstead (14) Dickens

CHELSEA 2 ARSENAL 1; February 2nd 1991 (Crowd 29,094) Scorers: Stuart Dixon; Smith

Against the backdrop of the Gulf War, the home team pulled off an historic triumph. Alan Smith's late effort was merely a consolation after young Graham Stuart and Kerry Dixon had scored the goals which would condemn the Gunners to their first and only league defeat in a truly remarkable campaign that provided the visitors with an emphatic League Championship victory. Luton Town were the only other team to score in both their league encounters with Arsenal, though Chelsea's tally of three goals was more than any other First Division club could manage. The north Londoners' success story was based on 29 clean sheets in league and cup collected by new goalkeeper David Seaman who shared the distinction of playing in all fifty league and cup matches with his trusted defenders Steve Bould, Lee Dixon and Nigel Winterburn. Only defeat in an FA Cup semi-final by a Paul Gascoigne-inspired Tottenham Hotspur spoiled Arsenal's season. The west Londoners meanwhile returned to mid-table mediocrity sandwiched between Tottenham Hotspur and Queen's Park Rangers. Consequently, Bobby Campbell would vacate the managerial seat in favour of 1973 FA Cup Final hero Ian Porterfield. In a throwback to the 1930s, defeating the mighty Arsenal was all that Chelsea had to crow about.

CHELSEA	ARSENAL
1 Beasant	1 Seaman
2 Hall	2 Dixon
3 Dorigo	3 Winterburn
4 Townsend	4 Thomas

5 Clarke	5	Bould (12)
Hillier		
6 Monkou	6 Linighan	
7 Le Saux (12) Bumstead	7 Groves	
8 Matthew	8 Davis	
9 Dixon (14) Wilson	9 Smith	
10 Stuart	10 Merson	
11 Wise	11 Limpar (14) Campbell	

SEASON 1990-1:
ARSENAL:
Finished 1st; Won 24; Drew 13; Lost 1; Goals for 74; Against 18; Points 83 (including 2 points deducted)
CHELSEA:
Finished 11th; Won 13; Drew 10; Lost 15; Goals for 58; Against 69; Points 49

ARSENAL 3 CHELSEA 2; October 5th 1991 (Crowd 42,074) Scorers: Dixon (Pen) Wright Campbell; Le Saux Wilson

In an extraordinary game, the home team (not for the last time) came from two goals behind to squeeze home for all three points. Goals from Graeme Le Saux and Northern Ireland's Kevin Wilson had laid the foundations for an upset, but a penalty from Lee Dixon and goals from Kevin Campbell and Ian Wright transformed a 2-1 half-time deficit into the reigning League Champions' fourth successive league triumph. Recent signing Ian Wright could 'only' manage one goal on his home debut after helping himself to a hat-trick in his first appearance at Southampton the previous Saturday. Chelsea would be one of many teams who would be on the receiving end in the ensuing years as Wright broke the goalscoring records at Arsenal. In the meantime, Wright and his team-mates were intent on making a stout defence of the league championship.

ARSENAL	CHELSEA
1 Seaman	1 Hitchcock
2 Dixon	2 Clarke
3 Winterburn	3 Boyd (12) Allon
4 Thomas	4 Jones
5 Linighan	5 Elliott
6 Pates	6 Monkou
7 Rocastle	7 Le Saux
8 Wright (14) O'Leary	8 Townsend
9 Smith	9 Dixon
10 Campbell	10 Wilson
11 Limpar (12) Merson	11 Wise

CHELSEA 1 ARSENAL 1; April 25th 1992 (Crowd 26,003) Scorers: Wise; Dixon

The Gunners were unable to successfully defend their League Championship, but they still finished as London's top team. The home team meanwhile seemed to be going backwards instead of forward. Anyhow, in their penultimate encounter of another disappointing campaign, the west Londoners at least restricted their visitors to a point. England internationals Lee Dixon and Dennis Wise each found the back of the net to ensure a sharing of the spoils. The next time Arsenal would visit Stamford Bridge;

Chelsea would have a 'new' man in charge – David Webb, the club's cup winning central defender.

CHELSEA	ARSENAL
1 Beasant	1 Seaman
2 Sinclair	2 Dixon
3 Le Saux	3 Winterburn
4 Jones	4 Hillier
5 Johnsen	5 Bould
6 Monkou (12) Hall	6 Adams
7 Stuart (14) Matthew	7 Rocastle
8 Townsend	8 Wright
9 Dixon	9 Campbell
10 Cascarino	10 Merson (14) O'Leary
11 Wise	11 Limpar (12) Smith

SEASON 1991-2:
ARSENAL:
Finished 4th; Won 19; Drew 15; Lost 8; Goals for 81; Against 46; Points 72
CHELSEA:
Finished 14th; Won 13; Drew 14; Lost 15; Goals for 50; Against 60; Points 53

ARSENAL 2 CHELSEA 1; October 3rd 1992 (Crowd 27,780) Scorers: Merson Wright; Wise

Before being substituted by Anders Limpar, Paul Merson had given the home team an early lead against the club he had supported as a youngster. Like his teammate Tony Adams, Merson had a roller coaster ride in his footballing career: scaling the heights with England international caps and collecting several medals with Arsenal, and plumbing the depths with alcohol and drug abuse. Dennis Wise, who would also fall foul of the law two years later, equalised in the second half, but Ian Wright (who himself was no angel) restored Arsenal's lead five minutes before the end of the contest. In spite of this triumph, the men in red were slipping into mid-table mediocrity.

ARSENAL	CHELSEA
Seaman	Hitchcock
Dixon	Hall
Winterburn	Sinclair
Hillier	Townsend
Bould	Lee
Adams	Donaghy (Stuart)
Jensen	Newton
Wright	Fleck
Smith	Harford
Merson (Limpar)	Spackman
Campbell	Wise

CHELSEA 1 ARSENAL 0; March 1st 1993 (Crowd 17,725) Scorer: Stuart

An encouraging run of form before Christmas gave rise to false hopes that Chelsea could mount a durable championship challenge. However, by the New Year the Blues had run out of steam with the result that Ian Porterfield was replaced as manager before this encounter. New boss David Webb in a brief stay at his old stamping ground at least presided over a narrow win against the north

Londoners. He had a late goal from Graham Stuart to thank for this victory as the much-maligned Dave Beasant collected another clean sheet against a team that peculiarly scored fewer goals in the new Premier League than any of the other twenty-one competitors. In spite of a toothless league campaign, George Graham's troops proceeded to win both the League Cup and the FA Cup against Sheffield Wednesday on each occasion.

CHELSEA	ARSENAL
Beasant	Seaman
Hall	Dixon
Sinclair	Morrow
Townsend	Hillier (Lydersen)
Johnsen	Linighan
Donaghy	Keown
Stuart	Jensen
Fleck	Campbell (Carter)
Harford (Spencer)	Smith
Newton	Merson
Barnard (Matthew)	Flatts

SEASON 1992-3:

ARSENAL:

Finished 10th; Won 15; Drew 11; Lost 16; Goals for 40; Against 38; Points 56

CHELSEA:

Finished 11th; Won 14; Drew 14; Lost 14; Goals for 51; Against 54; Points 56

CHELSEA 0 ARSENAL 2; November 20th 1993 (Crowd 26,839) Scorers: Smith Wright (Pen)

Former Tottenham Hotspur hero Glenn Hoddle was now occupying the managerial chair at Stamford Bridge, but on this day his charges slumped to their sixth successive defeat as the new man's immediate priority became that of navigating the west Londoners out of the perilous waters of the relegation zone. No strangers to scoring against hapless Chelsea, Alan Smith and Ian Wright inflicted the damage before the half-time interval as the home team failed to find the back of the net for the fourth time in their last five outings. The lethal Wright was en route to a season's total of 35 goals as Arsenal started to reassert themselves again.

CHELSEA	ARSENAL
Kharine	Seaman
Barnard	Dixon
Lee	Winterburn (Morrow)
Johnsen (Hopkin)	Davis
Sinclair	Keown
Peacock	Bould
Wise	Linighan
Clarke	Selley
Donaghy (Newton)	Merson
Shipperley	Wright
Stein	Smith

ARSENAL 1 CHELSEA 0; April 16th 1994 (Crowd 34,314)
Scorer: Wright

One week after the visitors had completed a successful FA Cup semi-final assignment at Wembley, they succumbed to the current FA Cup holders. An Ian Wright effort in the last twenty minutes of the contest separated the two teams thereby earning Arsenal their first league double against Chelsea since their double-winning year of 1971. The Blues at least had recovered from their relegation flirtations that were in evidence before Christmas, and they ultimately qualified for a place in Europe for the first time since 1971 on account of being FA Cup runners-up to double winners Manchester United. The Gunners followed up their domestic cup double of the previous season by landing the European Cup Winners' Cup in May of this year. Also worthy of note is that not only did David Seaman and his defence earn a shutout in their European final, but they became the first Arsenal contingent to collect a brace of clean sheets in a league season against Chelsea since 1978.

ARSENAL	CHELSEA
Seaman	Kharine
Dixon	Lee
Morrow	Sinclair
Hillier (Smith)	Spencer
Keown	Peacock
Adams	Wise
Selley	Clarke
Wright	Donaghy
Campbell	Newton
Parlour	Hopkin
McGoldrick	Kjeldbjerg

SEASON 1993-4:
ARSENAL:
Finished 4th; Won 18; Drew 17; Lost 7; Goals for 53; Against 28; Points 71

CHELSEA:
Finished 14th; Won 13; Drew 12; Lost 17; Goals for 49; Against 53; Points 51

ARSENAL 3 CHELSEA 1; October 15th 1994 (Crowd 38,234) Scorers: Wright (2) Campbell; Wise

Dennis Wise found the target again against the Gunners, but Ian Wright and Kevin Campbell turned the contest around with goals either side of half-time. Wright added a third as Chelsea's defensive frailties at corner kicks were exposed. The Blues, like their opponents, were engaged in a prolonged European adventure, but they remained as inconsistent as ever back home. In spite of this Arsenal triumph, they too endured a below par domestic season.

ARSENAL	CHELSEA
Seaman	Kharine
Dixon	Clarke
Bould	Kjeldbjerg
Adams (Keown)	Johnsen
Winterburn	Sinclair
Parlour	Rocastle (Shipperley)
Jensen (Selley)	Spackman
Schwarz	Peacock
Smith	Wise
Campbell	Furlong
Wright	Newton

CHELSEA 2 ARSENAL 1; May 14th 1995 (Crowd 29,542) Scorers: Furlong Stein; Hartson

Graham Rix made a surprise appearance as a substitute as he bowed out of professional football with this walk-on part against his former club. Although John Hartson cancelled out Paul Furlong's goal, Mark Stein restored the home team's lead early in the second half. As the curtains fell on a mediocre league campaign for both London clubs, all eyes were on the drama unfolding at Anfield and Upton Park as Blackburn Rovers edged home against Manchester United in the race for the Premier League. Meanwhile, both Chelsea and Arsenal (who had both been eliminated from the FA Cup in consecutive rounds by Millwall) narrowly missed out on European glory when they succumbed to Spanish team Real Zaragoza in the semi-finals and final of the European Cup Winners' Cup respectively. Glenn Hoddle, Chelsea manager, also hung up his boots after his last appearance here against his erstwhile footballing foes.

CHELSEA	ARSENAL
Kharine	Seaman
Clarke	Dixon
Sinclair	Adams
Lee	Bould
Minto	McGowan (Linighan)
Hopkins (Rix)	Merson
Hoddle (Burley)	Parlour
Spackman	Jensen
Peacock	Helder (Dickov)
Furlong	Hartson
Stein	Wright

SEASON 1994-5:

CHELSEA:
Finished 11th; Won 13; Drew 15; Lost 14; Goals for 50; Against 55; Points 54
ARSENAL:
Finished 12th; Won 13; Drew 12; Lost 17; Goals for 52; Against 49; Points 51

CHELSEA 1 ARSENAL 0; September 30th 1995 (Crowd 31,048) Scorer: Hughes

With the help of new funds from the late Matthew Harding, a new revolution was unfolding at Stamford Bridge. Superstar Ruud Gullit had been signed in the close season, and it was another Hoddle signing Mark Hughes whose goal shortly after half-time decided the outcome of this fiercely contested derby encounter. The home team hung for victory in spite of being reduced to ten men after Nigel Spackman was uncharacteristically sent off five minutes before the final whistle. Although the home team had now twice beaten Arsenal in the same year for the first time since 1970, the anticipated progress on the league front was not forthcoming

CHELSEA	ARSENAL
Kharine	Seaman
Burley	Dixon
Johnsen	Adams
Sinclair	Bould (Linighan)
Myers	Winterburn
Gullit	Parlour
Spackman	Keown
Peacock (Newton)	Jensen (Helder)

Wise	Merson
Hughes	Bergkamp
Furlong	Wright

ARSENAL 1 CHELSEA 1; December 16th 1995 (Crowd 38,295) Scorers: Dixon; Spencer

Having overcome runaway league leaders Newcastle United in the previous weekend, the visitors continued their revival with an excellent performance at Highbury which almost yielded a rare win. Pint-sized Scottish striker John Spencer, fit again after a long lay-off, put the away team in front halfway through the first half. Dan Petrescu, a recent signing and goalscoring hero against the Magpies, missed a golden opportunity to wrap up the points, but with Steve Bould receiving his marching orders, an away win seemed almost certain. However, when the Blues failed to effectively clear a corner kick, Lee Dixon rifled a speculative effort beyond Dmitri Kharine to rob Chelsea of all three points. However, with Manchester United obtaining their second double in three years, neither London club would be redecorating their trophy cabinets with more silverware.

ARSENAL	CHELSEA
Seaman	Kharine
Dixon	Petrescu
Bould	Burley
Adams	Lee
Winterburn	Phelan (Clarke)
Merson	Myers
Keown	Newton

Platt	Wise
Hartson	Duberry
Wright	Spencer (Furlong)
Jensen (Helder)	Hughes

SEASON 1995-6:
ARSENAL:
Finished 5th; Won 17; Drew 12; Lost 9; Goals for 49; Against 32; Points 63
CHELSEA:
Finished 11th; Won 12; Drew 14; Lost 12; Goals for 46; Against 44; Points 50

ARSENAL 3 CHELSEA 3; September 4th 1996 (Crowd 38,132) Scorers: Merson Keown Wright; Leboeuf (Pen) Vialli Wise

With the successful George Graham era coming to a controversial end, Arsenal was in transition. On the eve of Arsène Wenger's appointment as new "coach," Chelsea took advantage of the interregnum at Highbury to lay the foundations for a possible triumph. Recent signing Franck Leboeuf converted the first of many successful spot kicks, and another new signing, Italian superstar Gianluca Vialli doubled the lead as the Blues profited from the absence of David Seaman. Paul Merson fired home a goal just before half- time to throw the Gunners a lifeline they scarcely deserved. In the second half, Martin Keown scored from a corner kick while half-time substitute Ian Wright lobbed the advancing Dmitri Kharine to present the home team with the lead. However, John Spencer found Dennis Wise who duly obliged with a last gasp equaliser. This breathless contest had seen both teams throw away winning positions and come back from seemingly hopeless positions. It is hard to know which club was more satisfied with the final result!

ARSENAL	CHELSEA
Lukic	Kharine
Dixon	Petrescu
Winterburn	Leboeuf (Duberry)
Bould (Wright)	Clarke
Merson	Myers
Bergkamp	Vialli
Linighan	Hughes
Keown	Wise
Parlour	Burley (Spencer)
Hartson	Di Matteo
Morrow (Platt)	Johnsen

CHELSEA 0 ARSENAL 3; April 5th 1997 (Crowd 28,182)
Scorers: Wright Platt Bergkamp

Experienced international trio Dennis Bergkamp, David Platt, and Ian Wright provided the goals as the visitors put their hosts to the sword. In mitigation, Ruud Gullit rested a few players in preparation for a semi-final date with Wimbledon at Highbury in the FA Cup in eight days' time. Consequently, the Gunners cruised to victory against a young, patched up home team. The west Londoners would have the last laugh as they proceeded to lift the FA Cup six weeks later for the second time in Chelsea's history to make amends for finishing below Arsenal in the league again. This match had been a morning kick-off on Grand

National day, but a bomb-scare meant that the main event at Aintree had to be postponed for two days.

CHELSEA	ARSENAL
Grodas	Seaman
Petrescu	Dixon
Clarke	Winterburn
Burley	Vieira (Selley)
Minto (Nicholls)	Bould
Johnsen (Granville)	Platt
Parker (Myers)	Wright (Anelka)
Morris	Bergkamp
P Hughes	Keown
Zola	Garde
Vialli	S Hughes (Parlour)

SEASON 1996-7:
ARSENAL:
Finished 3rd; Won 19; Drew 11; Lost 8; Goals for 62; Against 32; Points 68
CHELSEA:
Finished 6th; Won 16; Drew 11; Lost 11; Goals for 58; Against 55; Points 59

CHELSEA 2 ARSENAL 3; September 21st 1997 (Crowd 31,549) Scorers: Poyet Zola; Bergkamp (2) Winterburn

The first of four showdowns between these two teams in a historic season for both clubs ended in a narrow triumph for the away team. New signing Gustavo Poyet hooked the ball home from close range to open the scoring five minutes before the break. However, just before the interval, Dennis Bergkamp had restored parity, before going on to give Arsenal the lead fifteen minutes into the second half. With defensive frailties being exposed at both ends of the field, Gianfranco Zola was able to record his first goal of the season almost immediately after the home team had gone behind. The outcome of this typically frenetic duel was influenced by the sending off of Franck Leboeuf who, like his team-mates, could not cope with Dennis Bergkamp. The Blues looked as if they could cling on to a point until up stepped Nigel Winterburn to unleash an unstoppable thirty yard shot in the dying minutes. Not for the first or last time, Arsenal had saved the best for last.

CHELSEA	ARSENAL
De Goey	Seaman
P Hughes	Dixon
Le Saux	Winterburn
Duberry	Adams
Leboeuf	Bould
Di Matteo (Flo)	Overmars
Petrescu (Nicholls)	Parlour
Poyet	Petit
Wise	Vieira
Vialli (M Hughes)	Bergkamp
Zola	Wright

ARSENAL 2 CHELSEA 1; January 28th 1998 (Crowd 38,114) League Cup Semi-Final 1st Leg; Scorers: Overmars S Hughes; M Hughes

A Wembley final in March beckoned for either club after the two London rivals were drawn together in the League Cup for the first time since 1976. The result from then was repeated this time as the home team completely outplayed the visitors virtually from start to finish. Dutch winger Marc Overmars furnished Arsenal with the lead halfway through the first half, before young Stephen Hughes extended the apparent gap between the two protagonists in the first minute of the second half. However, another Hughes, the 'Sparky' variety, had the final say as the fiery Welshman headed the visitors back into contention. A big improvement would be required by the Blues in the second tie if they were to progress any further. As for Arsenal they should have had the contest dead and buried.

ARSENAL	CHELSEA
Manninger	De Goey
Grimandi (Platt)	Clarke
Winterburn	Sinclair (Vialli)
Adams	Duberry
Bould	Gullit
S Hughes	Lambourde
Overmars	Le Saux
Parlour	Newton
Petit	Petrescu (Charvet)
Anelka	Flo (M Hughes)
Bergkamp	Zola

ARSENAL 2 CHELSEA 0; February 8th 1998 (Crowd 38,083) Scorer: S Hughes (2)

Stephen Hughes took his goal tally against Chelsea to three in just eleven days as the away team capitulated against fast-improving Arsenal for the third time. Hughes had scored at each end of the first half, profiting first from an under-hit Leboeuf back pass and then popping up in the right place from a free kick which Tony Adams had headed into his path. Rumours abound that Ruud Gullit literally banged his head against the wall at half-time in frustration at the events that had unfolded. Whatever the truth, Gullit's previous encounter with Arsenal marked the end of his illustrious professional playing career, while this contest with Arsenal would be his last outing as Chelsea manager. A financial dispute over salary negotiations obliged the Chelsea board to replace Ruud Gullit with one of his signings – Gianluca Vialli. The Blues were still riding high in the league and actively involved in pursuing two cups, but the dreadlocked Dutchman was nevertheless shown the exit door. The Gunners meanwhile went from strength to strength to claim their third league title in ten years.

ARSENAL	CHELSEA
Manninger	De Goey
Grimandi (Dixon)	Charvet
Winterburn	Le Saux
Adams	Duberry
Bould	Leboeuf
S Hughes	Di Matteo
Overmars (Platt)	Newton (Flo)
Parlour	Petrescu (Granville)
Petit	Wise
Anelka (Wright)	M Hughes
Bergkamp	Vialli (Zola)

CHELSEA 3 ARSENAL 1; February 18th 1998 (Crowd 34,430) League Cup Semi-Final 2nd Leg; Scorers: M Hughes Di Matteo Petrescu; Bergkamp (Pen)

Shock appointment Gianluca Vialli hit the ground running with an outstanding victory against Arsenal that enabled Chelsea to progress to the Coca Cola Cup Final where they beat Middlesbrough 2-0 again in a Wembley final. Vialli threw caution to the wind somewhat by employing a 4-3-3 formation, and his strategy was vindicated after Mark Hughes (again) thumped home a goal inside ten minutes to turn the contest on its head. The visitors suffered a traumatic opening quarter of an hour in the second half during which Roberto Di Matteo produced one of his trademark run and shoot efforts, closely followed by an exquisite finish from the edge of the box by Rumanian international Dan Petrescu. As if this was not bad enough for the Gunners, Patrick Vieira was sent off, but the men in red in spite of this handicap exerted much pressure in the closing quarter of an hour with Dennis Bergkamp converting a penalty, but the west Londoners hung on for victory. It would be a glorious spring for both clubs as the Blues lifted the European Cup Winners' Cup for the second time, but this vintage year for Chelsea hardly compares with Arsenal's stunning league and cup double triumph which towered over Chelsea's successes.

CHELSEA	ARSENAL
De Goey	Manninger
Clarke	Dixon
Le Saux	Winterburn(S.Hughes)

Duberry	Adams
Leboeuf	Grimandi
Di Matteo	Overmars
Petrescu	Parlour (Platt)
Wise	Petit
M Hughes	Vieira
Vialli (Newton)	Anelka
Zola	Bergkamp

SEASON 1997-8:
ARSENAL:
Finished 1st; Won 23; Drew 9; Lost 6; Goals for 68; Against 33; Points 78

CHELSEA:
Finished 4th; Won 20; Drew 3; Lost 15; Goals for 71; Against 43; Points 63

CHELSEA 0 ARSENAL 0; September 9th 1998 (Crowd 34,644)
Fresh from their European Super Cup humbling of the mighty Real Madrid, Chelsea held the reigning League Champions to a point. The away team were probably more satisfied with their hard-won point after they had been restricted to ten men following Lee Dixon's sending off with a full half hour to play. Danish international winger Brian Laudrup made his debut league appearance, but failed to live up to the pre-match hype. David Seaman and his defence kept the home team at bay, thus signalling Arsenal's resolve to hold on to their Premier League trophy

against the likes of Chelsea and more ominously Manchester United.

CHELSEA	ARSENAL
De Goey	Seaman
Babayaro	Dixon
Leboeuf	Winterburn
Desailly	Vieira
Laudrup (Poyet)	Adams
Casiraghi	Anelka (S Hughes)
Duberry	Bergkamp (Wreh)
Le Saux	Overmars (Garde)
Di Matteo	Keown
Lambourde (Petrescu)	Parlour
Zola (Flo)	Petit

ARSENAL 0 CHELSEA 5; November 11th 1998 (Crowd 37,562) League Cup 4th Round; Scorers: Leboeuf (Pen) Vialli (2) Poyet (2)

The fifth meeting of the year between these two clubs resulted in a stupendous triumph for the League Cup holders against the reigning FA Cup champions. Franck Leboeuf opened the scoring with another successful spot-kick, but few at half-time could have envisaged the avalanche of goals that would follow as Gustavo Poyet and player-coach Luca Vialli helped themselves to doubles. New signing Bjarne Goldbaek made a satisfactory start to his brief Chelsea career, having brought in as a replacement for the departed Brian Laudrup. Arsène Wenger claimed that his team did not take this cup tie seriously, but another large crowd at Highbury suggested that they at least took this encounter seriously. Anyhow, after achieving their biggest ever win in peacetime over the Gunners, the west Londoners almost predictably failed to match this performance away to Wimbledon and so they bowed out 2-1. Yet again, beating Arsenal appeared to be Chelsea's 'cup final.'

ARSENAL	CHELSEA
Manninger	Kharine
Vivas	Petrescu
Ljungberg	Babayaro
Bergkamp (Cabellero)	Leboeuf (Lambourde)
Wreh	Goldbaek (Percassi)
S Hughes	Poyet
Garde (Mendez)	Vialli
Grimandi	Duberry
Upson	Di Matteo
Boa Morte	Flo
Grondin	Nicholls (Clement)

ARSENAL 1 CHELSEA 0; January 31st 1999 (Crowd 38,121) Scorer: Bergkamp

A moment of genius from Dennis Bergkamp decided the outcome of this closely contested derby, which was the eighth successive fixture between the two giants to be screened live – a testimony to the increasing significance of this local skirmish. Young Finnish striker Mikkel Forssell made his first appearance for the away team, but he could not prevent Chelsea's first league defeat since the opening day of the season. Luca Vialli's foreign legion would suffer only one more league defeat (in another derby fixture against West Ham United) as the boys in blue reached their highest league position since 1970. Like Arsenal, Chelsea's season was a story of what might have been, as both London clubs were knocked out of the latter stages of the FA Cup by Manchester United, who also beat them to the Premier League finishing line. At least the two London clubs could share in the prospect of competing in the Champions League, which the Red Devils also won in 1999.

ARSENAL	CHELSEA
Seaman	De Goey
Dixon	Petrescu
Winterburn	Babayaro
Adams	Leboeuf
Anelka (Vivas)	Desailly
Bergkamp (Upson)	Vialli
Overmars (Diawara)	Wise
Keown	Duberry (Goldbaek)
Parlour	Le Saux
Petit	Di Matteo
Garde	Zola (Forsell)

SEASON 1998-9:
ARSENAL:
Finished 2nd; Won 22; Drew 12; Lost 4; Goals for 59; Against 17; Points 78
CHELSEA:
Finished 3rd; Won 20; Drew 15; Lost 3; Goals for 57; Against 30; Points 75

CHELSEA 2 ARSENAL 3; October 23rd 1999 (Crowd 34,958) Scorers: Flo Petrescu; Kanu (3)

Fittingly, the last duel between two of London's finest in the twentieth century ended in a dramatic victory for the Gunners. Headed efforts either side of halftime by Tore Andre Flo and Dan Petrescu put the home team firmly on course for three points. That is, until Nigerian international Nwankwo Kanu conjured up a remarkable hat-trick in the last quarter of an hour. Kanu's last gasp winner was converted from a narrow angle as Ed De Goey and Franck Leboeuf mysteriously swapped defensive and goalkeeping duties. The Blues had hammered English and European champions Manchester United 5-0 at the same venue three weeks earlier, but their domestic fortunes were becoming increasingly undermined by an impressive run in the Champions League. Kanu's trio of goals was the first in this derby fixture since Bobby Tambling in 1964.

CHELSEA	ARSENAL
De Goey	Seaman
Ferrer	Dixon
Le Saux (Poyet)	Silvinho
Deschamps	Petit (Vieira)
Leboeuf	Keown
Desailly	Adams
Petrescu	Parlour
Babayaro	Ljungberg (Henry)
Sutton	Suker
Flo (Zola)	Kanu
Wise	Overmars (Vernazza)

ARSENAL 2 CHELSEA 1; May 6th 2000 (Crowd 38,119)
Scorers: Henry (2); Poyet

A double from flying Frenchman Thierry Henry set the hosts on their way to another league double over the west Londoners. Uruguayan midfielder Gustavo Poyet came off the bench to score, but the men in red were not to be denied. Nevertheless, the losers could at least console themselves with the prospect of another FA Cup Final appointment – this time with Aston Villa. Yet again the Blues had played second fiddle to Arsenal in the league, but victory in the cup final made amends for this, as Chelsea squeezed into the UEFA Cup.

ARSENAL	CHELSEA
Seaman	De Goey
Dixon	Melchiot
Silvinho	Lambourde
Vieira	Morris (Deschamps)
Grimandi	Leboeuf (Thome)
Adams	Desailly
Parlour	Zola (Poyet)
Henry	Di Matteo
Petit (Luzhny)	Flo
Bergkamp	Weah
Overmars (Winterburn)	Wise

SEASON 1999-2000:
ARSENAL:
Finished 2nd; Won 22; Drew 7; Lost 9; Goals for 73; Against 43; Points 73

CHELSEA:
Finished 5th; Won 18; Drew 11; Lost 9; Goals for 53; Against 34; Points 65

CHELSEA 2 ARSENAL 2; September 6th 2000 (Crowd 34,924) Scorers: Hasselbaink Zola; Henry Silvinho

Arsenal's never-say-die approach was in evidence once more after the home team had opened up a two goals cushion with only half an hour left to play. New signing Jimmy Floyd Hasselbaink continued his rich vein of scoring against Arsenal from his Leeds United days while Gianfranco Zola doubled the lead fifteen minutes into the second half. Again, Arsène Wenger's troops resolved to do things the hard way and proceeded belatedly to throw the kitchen sink at their hosts. The home fans must have despaired as Chelsea capitulated once again in the face of Arsenal's eleventh hour onslaught. Thierry Henry's goal a quarter of an hour before the end would have been little more than a consolation had it not been for another last gasp wonder strike from Gunners' left-back Silvinho, who in the tradition of full backs Dixon and Winterburn, ensured that Arsenal predictably would have the last word.

CHELSEA
Cudicini
Panucci
Babayaro
Leboeuf
Desailly
Le Saux
Wise

ARSENAL
Seaman
Dixon (Wiltord)
Keown
Silvinho
Grimandi
Luzhny
Pires (Ljungberg)

Poyet (Melchiot)	Lauren
Di Matteo	Parlour(Bergkamp)
Hasselbaink	Henry
Zola (Morris)	Kanu

ARSENAL 1 CHELSEA 1; January 13th 2001 (Crowd 38,071) Scorers: Pires; Terry

The Gunners altered the script for this mid-winter fixture by taking the lead inside the first five minutes. French international winger Robert Pires, who had previously scored against Chelsea in a Champions' League engagement for Olympique Marseilles, fired the home team in front, but with Claudio Ranieri now in charge of the Blues, the away team changed players and tactics at half-time to transform the contest. With Danish international winger Jesper Gronkjaer making his first appearance for the west Londoners in place of Slavisa Jokanovic at the start of the second half, the away team started to assert themselves. A much improved second half performance from the visitors found its reward when promising young centre-half John Terry put Chelsea level from a corner kick. Also replaced at the interval was Frank Leboeuf who was becoming increasingly out of favour at 'the Bridge.' Arsenal meanwhile would be presented with another opportunity to show who's boss when they were obliged by the FA Cup draw to host the FA Cup champions in a fifth round clash in five weeks time.

ARSENAL	CHELSEA
Seaman	Cudicini
Dixon	Leboeuf (Ferrer)

Stepanovs	Desailly
Keown	Dalla Bona
Silvinho	Terry
Pires	Jokanovic (Gronkjaer)
Ljungberg	Poyet
Parlour	Wise
Vieira	Harley
Wiltord	Gudjohnsen (Zola)
Henry	Hasselbaink

ARSENAL 3 CHELSEA 1; February 18th 2001 (Crowd 38,096) FA Cup 5th Round Scorers: Henry (Pen) Wiltord (2); Hasselbaink

The London giants' first FA Cup encounter since 1973 proved a happy occasion for French pair Thierry Henry and Sylvain Wiltord who shared three goals between them in the destruction of the Blues. After Henry had converted from the spot, Hasselbaink, who finished the season as top scorer in the league with 23 goals, responded with a stunning strike. The scene was then set for 'supersub' Wiltord to restore the lead and seal victory with two goals. The Gunners would progress to the first final at Cardiff's Millennium Stadium where they uncharacteristically threw their lead away to a Michael Owen-inspired Liverpool. Accustomed to the regular acquisition of silverware, there were rumblings of discontent at Highbury that Arsenal had narrowly failed for the third consecutive year to win any honours. Chelsea meanwhile remained as inconsistent as ever.

ARSENAL	CHELSEA

Seaman	Cudicini
Dixon	Babayaro
Stepanovs	Desailly
Luzhny	Ferrer (Stanic)
Cole	Dalla Bona(Gronkjaer)
Ljungberg	Terry
Lauren	Poyet
Vieira	Wise
Pires (Wiltord)	Jokanovic
Bergkamp	Zola (Gudjohnsen)
Henry	Hasselbaink

SEASON 2000-1:
ARSENAL:
Finished 2nd; Won 20; Drew 10; Lost 8; Goals for 63; Against 38; Points 70
CHELSEA:
Finished 6th; Won 17; Drew 10; Lost 11; Goals for 68; Against 45; Points 61

CHELSEA 1 ARSENAL 1; September 8th 2001 (Crowd 40,855) Scorers: Hasselbaink (Pen); Henry

Arguably the two best strikers in the Premier League each contributed a goal as the spoils were shared for the third consecutive league match between the two. Thierry Henry gave the visitors a deserved lead before Jimmy Floyd Hasselbaink brought the teams level from the penalty spot. In the second half, the home team held on for a point, in spite of the sending off of Hasselbaink for a less than legal challenge on Martin Keown. Hasselbaink had the distinction of being sent off twice in the season against

North London's big two and having each red card overturned on appeal. Henry meanwhile narrowly pipped Hasselbaink as the top league goalscorer with a double at home to Everton on the final day of the season, leaving him with 24 goals, one more than the controversial Dutchman. Remarkably, although Arsenal struggled to find any form on their travels in the Champions League, they progressed through an impressive league campaign unbeaten away from home, having scored in every one of their 38 league outings.

CHELSEA	ARSENAL
De Goey	Seaman
Desailly	Cole
Gallas	Keown
Terry	Adams (Campbell)
Le Saux	Grimandi
Lampard	Lauren
Petit	Van Bronckhorst
Zenden (Melchiot)	Pires
Gronkjaer (Stanic)	Henry
Hasselbaink	Wiltord (Ljungberg)
Zola	Bergkamp (Kanu)

ARSENAL 2 CHELSEA 1; December 26th 2001 (38,079)
Scorers: Campbell Wiltord; Lampard

In an extraordinary month for the away team, they suffered their second narrow defeat in a London derby (Charlton Athletic predictably were the other victors). On the other hand, the Blues had successfully despatched Newcastle United both home and away as well as thrashing Liverpool

4-0 and winning 3-0 at Manchester United. While the west Londoners remained brilliantly unpredictable, doubts were cast upon Arsenal's Premiership aspirations, after having been humbled at home 4-2 and 3-1 by Charlton Athletic and Newcastle United respectively. Anyhow, the Gunners demonstrated their character once again by overturning a 1-0 half-time deficit. Former West Ham United midfielder Frank Lampard had burst into the home team's penalty area and sweetly planted his shot beyond the goalkeeper's despairing dive just before the interval. A subdued Arsenal was revived by ex-Tottenham Hotspur central defender Sol Campbell who firmly headed home a corner kick soon after the break. A close contest was then decided by a shot from Sylvain Wiltord, who duly scored his third goal against Chelsea in 2001 at Highbury. With Manchester United suffering a pre-Christmas dip in form and Leeds United going into free-fall in the New Year, the scene was set for another Premier League triumph for Arsène Wenger's troops.

ARSENAL	CHELSEA
Taylor	Cudicini
Lauren	Melchiot
Keown	Terry
Campbell	Gallas
Cole	Babayaro
Ljungberg (Wiltord)	Le Saux (Zola)
Parlour (Van Bronckhorst)	Stanic (Dalla Bona)
Vieira	Lampard
Pires	Petit
Kanu (Bergkamp)	Gudjohnsen (Forsell)
Henry	Hasselbaink

ARSENAL 2 CHELSEA 0; May 4th 2002 (Crowd 73,963)
FA Cup Final; Scorers: Parlour Ljungberg

After having unconvincingly negotiated their semi-finals by one goal to nil, London's top two teams went to Cardiff to compete in the first all-London final for twenty years. Given the fact that these two clubs have featured prominently in the FA Cup over the last decade, it was almost inevitable that they would eventually collide in a final. After all, of the last ten FA Cup Finals either Arsenal or Chelsea had appeared in no fewer then seven dating back to 1993. The Gunners were allocated the 'lucky' dressing room, and so it proved. Most neutral observers could have been forgiven for feeling disappointed that the huge array of talent on display did not produce the exciting spectacle that had been anticipated. David Seaman made his first FA Cup appearance of the season, and ably assisted by fellow England internationals the redoubtable Tony Adams and Sol Campbell, he duly collected another clean sheet against the west Londoners. Frank Lampard and Graeme Le Saux were restricted to long range shots while Jesper Gronkjaer fired weakly at Seaman in the first half. Only an excellent curling effort from Eidur Gudjohnsen after the break really extended the dependable Seaman. The men in red came close to scoring in the first half when Dennis Bergkamp headed wide, when well placed. After the interval, when the Blues ironically were beginning to assert themselves, the deadlock was finally broken. Moments after the half-fit Jimmy Floyd Hasselbaink had been replaced by Gianfranco Zola, Ray Parlour strode forward and unleashed a stunning strike which would have graced any final. Swedish international midfielder, Freddie Ljungberg, who was enjoying an end of season goals harvest, confirmed Arsenal's superiority with another well-taken finish. Four days later and Arsène Wenger's team completed the other half of an historic league and cup double by triumphing 1-0 at Old Trafford against erstwhile foes Manchester United.

ARSENAL	CHELSEA
Seaman	Cudicini
Lauren	Melchiot (Zenden)
Cole	Babayaro (Terry)
Adams	Desailly
Campbell	Gallas
Vieira	Lampard
Parlour	Le Saux
Ljungberg	Petit
Wiltord (Keown)	Gronkjaer
Bergkamp (Edu)	Gudjohnsen
Henry (Kanu)	Hasselbaink (Zola)

SEASON 2001-2:
ARSENAL:
Finished 1st; Won 26; Drew 9; Lost 3; Goals for 79; Against 36; Points 87
CHELSEA:
Finished 6th; Won 17; Drew 13; Lost 8; Goals for 66; Against 38; Points 64

CHELSEA 1 ARSENAL 1; September 1st 2002 (Crowd 40,037) Scorers: Zola; Toure

In a re-run of the 2002 FA Cup Final, the reigning double winners left Stamford Bridge with a well-earned point. In a game ruined by over-zealous refereeing, Gianfranco Zola presented the home team with the half-time lead courtesy of a goal direct from a free kick which deceived David Seaman. Chelsea should have profited from the harsh sending off of Patrick Vieira at the beginning of the second half, but instead it was the away team who responded to the challenge, and they obtained their reward when Ivory Coast substitute Kolo Toure scored from close range. The 150th league and cup derby encounter between the two London giants ended with Arsenal yet again proving to be near impossible to defeat as Chelsea remain in search of their first league victory against the Gunners since 1995.

CHELSEA	ARSENAL
Cudicini	Seaman
Ferrer	Lauren
Le Saux (Melchiot)	Cole
Desailly	Campbell
Gallas	Keown
De Lucas	Edu (Toure)
Lampard	Gilberto Silva
Gronkjaer	Parlour
Zenden (Stanic)	Vieira
Gudjohnsen	Kanu
Zola (Hasselbaink)	Wiltord (Aliadiere)

Arsenal vs Chelsea

APPENDIX

Table 1: The first 150 League and Cup games (1907-2002)
Arsenal Won 62; Drew 45; Lost 43; Goals for 221; Against 186
Chelsea won 43; Drew 45; Lost 62; Goals for 186; Against 221

Table 2: The War Time Encounters
First World War:
Arsenal Won 6; Lost 10; Goals for 24; Against 43
Chelsea won 10; Lost 6; Goals for 43; Against 24
Second World War:
Arsenal Won 6; Drew 1; Lost 6; Goals for 30; Against 23
Chelsea Won 6; Drew 1: Lost 6; Goals for 23; Against 30

Table 3: Highest Attendance Figures
1. CHELSEA 1 ARSENAL 1; 12th OCTOBER 1935 (82,905)
2. CHELSEA 2 ARSENAL 2; 9th OCTOBER 1937 (75,952)
3. CHELSEA 1 ARSENAL 5; 29th NOVEMBER 1930 (74,667)
4. CHELSEA 1 ARSENAL 3; 22nd APRIL 1933 (74,190)
5. ARSENAL 2 CHELSEA 0; 4th MAY 2002 (73,963) at the Millennium Stadium, Cardiff.
6. CHELSEA 1 ARSENAL 1; 3rd APRIL 1953 (72,614)
7. CHELSEA 1 ARSENAL 1; 11th JANUARY 1947 (70,257)
8. ARSENAL 1 CHELSEA 1; 5th APRIL 1952 (68,084) at White Hart Lane.

9. ARSENAL 2 CHELSEA 2; 18th MARCH 1950 (67,752) at White Hart Lane.

10. CHELSEA 0 ARSENAL 0; 1st NOVEMBER 1947 (67,277)

Table 4: Highest Scoring Derby Encounters
1. ARSENAL 5 CHELSEA 4; 8th MARCH 1958
2= CHELSEA 2 ARSENAL 5; 24th NOVEMBER 1934
2= ARSENAL 5 CHELSEA 2; 16th APRIL 1979
4= CHELSEA 1 ARSENAL 5; 29th NOVEMBER 1930
4= CHELSEA 4 ARSENAL 2; 15th OCTOBER 1938
4= ARSENAL 2 CHELSEA 4; 14th MARCH 1964
4= ARSENAL 3 CHELSEA 3; 4th SEPTEMBER 1996

Table 5: The FA Cup Games
JANUARY 30th 1915 CHELSEA 1 WOOLWICH ARSENAL 0
JANUARY 11th 1930 ARSENAL 2 CHELSEA 0
JANUARY 24th 1931 CHELSEA 2 ARSENAL 1
JANUARY 7th 1939 CHELSEA 2 ARSENAL 1
JANUARY 11th 1947 CHELSEA 1 ARSENAL 1
JANUARY 15th 1947 ARSENAL 1 CHELSEA 1 after extra time.
JANUARY 20th 1947 ARSENAL 0 CHELSEA 2 at White Hart Lane
MARCH 18th 1950 ARSENAL 2 CHELSEA 2 at White Hart Lane.
MARCH 22nd 1950 ARSENAL 1 CHELSEA 0 after extra time at White Hart Lane.
APRIL 5th 1952 ARSENAL 1 CHELSEA 1 at White Hart Lane.

APRIL 7th 1952 ARSENAL 3 CHELSEA 0 at White Hart Lane.
MARCH 17th 1973 CHELSEA 2 ARSENAL 2
MARCH 20th 1973 ARSENAL 2 CHELSEA 1
FEBRUARY 18th 2001 ARSENAL 3 CHELSEA 1
MAY 4th 2002 ARSENAL 2 CHELSEA 0 at the Millennium Stadium, Cardiff.

Table 6: The League Cup Games
OCTOBER 26th 1976 ARSENAL 2 CHELSEA 1
JANUARY 28th 1998 ARSENAL 2 CHELSEA 1
FEBRUARY 18th 1998 CHELSEA 3 ARSENAL 1
NOVEMBER 11th 1998 ARSENAL 0 CHELSEA 5

Table 7: Leading Scorers
CLIFF BASTIN (ARSENAL) 10 GOALS
BOBBY TAMBLING (CHELSEA) 10 GOALS

Table 9: The Managers
ARSENAL:
1894-97: SAM HOLLIS
1897-98: TOM MITCHELL
1898-99: GEORGE ELCOAT
1899-1904: HARRY BRADSHAW
1904-08: PHIL KELSO
1908-15: GEORGE MORRELL
1919-25: LESLIE KNIGHTON
1925-34: HERBERT CHAPMAN
1934-47: GEORGE ALLISON
1947-56: TOM WHITTAKER
1956-58: JACK CRAYSTON
1958-62: GEORGE SWINDIN

1962-66: BILLY WRIGHT
1966-76: BERTIE MEE
1976-83: TERRY NEILL
1984-86: DON HOWE
1986-95: GEORGE GRAHAM
1995-96: BRUCE RIOCH
1996- : ARSÈNE WENGER

CHELSEA:
1905-06: JOHN TAIT ROBERTSON
1907-33: DAVID CALDERHEAD
1933-39: LESLIE KNIGHTON
1939-52: BILLY BIRRELL
1952-61: TED DRAKE
1962-67 TOMMY DOCHERTY
1967-74: DAVE SEXTON
1974-75: RON SUART
1975-77: EDDIE McCREADIE
1977-78: KEN SHELLITO
1978-79: DANNY BLANCHFLOWER
1979-81: GEOFF HURST
1981-85: JOHN NEAL
1985-88: JOHN HOLLINS
1988-91: BOBBY CAMPBELL
1991-93: IAN PORTERFIELD
1993-93: DAVID WEBB
1993-96: GLENN HODDLE
1996-98: RUUD GULIT
1998-2000: GIANLUCA VIALLI
2000- : CLAUDIO RANIERI

Table 10: Major Honour's List
ARSENAL:
1926: DIVISION ONE RUNNERS-UP
1927: FA CUP RUNNERS-UP
1930: FA CUP WINNERS
1931: DIVISION ONE CHAMPIONS
1932: DIVISION ONE RUNNERS-UP + FA CUP RUNNERS-UP
1933: DIVISION ONE CHAMPIONS
1934: DIVISION ONE CHAMPIONS
1935: DIVISION ONE CHAMPIONS
1936: FA CUP WINNERS
1938: DIVISION ONE CHAMPIONS
1948: DIVISION ONE CHAMPIONS
1950: FA CUP WINNERS
1952: FA CUP RUNNERS-UP
1953: DIVISION ONE CHAMPIONS
1968: LEAGUE CUP RUNNERS-UP
1969: LEAGUE CUP RUNNERS-UP
1970: FAIRS CUP WINNERS
1971: DIVISION ONE CHAMPIONS + FA CUP WINNERS
1972: FA CUP RUNNERS-UP
1973: DIVISION ONE RUNNERS-UP
1978: FA CUP RUNNERS-UP
1979: FA CUP WINNERS
1980: FA CUP RUNNERS-UP + CUP WINNERS' CUP RUNNERS-UP
1987: LEAGUE CUP WINNERS
1988: LEAGUE CUP RUNNERS-UP
1989: DIVISION ONE CHAMPIONS
1991: DIVISION ONE CHAMPIONS

1993: FA CUP + LEAGUE CUP WINNERS
1994: CUP WINNERS' CUP CHAMPIONS
1995: CUP WINNERS' CUP RUNNERS-UP
1998: PREMIER LEAGUE CHAMPIONS + FA CUP WINNERS
1999: PREMIER LEAGUE RUNNERS-UP
2000: PREMIER LEAGUE RUNNERS-UP + UEFA CUP RUNNERS-UP
2001: PREMIER LEAGUE RUNNERS-UP + FA CUP RUNNERS-UP
2002: PREMIER LEAGUE CHAMPIONS + FA CUP WINNERS

CHELSEA:
1916: FA CUP RUNNERS-UP
1955: DIVISION ONE CHAMPIONS
1965: LEAGUE CUP WINNERS
1967: FA CUP RUNNERS-UP
1970: FA CUP WINNERS
1971: CUP WINNER' CUP CHAMPIONS
1972: LEAGUE CUP RUNNERS-UP
1994: FA CUP RUNNERS-UP
1997: FA CUP WINNERS
1998: LEAGUE CUP WINNERS + CUP WINNERS' CUP CHAMPIONS
2000: FA CUP WINNERS
2002: FA CUP RUNNERS-UP

WAR TIME DERBY ENCOUNTERS (1915-1919)

When war was declared by Asquith's Liberal Government in August 1914, it was assumed by most people that the hostilities would be over by Christmas. However, when stalemate set in and the conflict extended into 1915, it became clear that normal league football would be obliged to suspend its activities for the duration of the national emergency. Consequently, with the onset of total war in which the British people had to serve in the essential services (such as farming and the armaments industry) as well as pick up rifles when conscription took effect, then domestic football had to hastily re-organise.

For Arsenal and Chelsea, new competitions were introduced to keep the London clubs occupied, but with all teams experiencing constant changes in personnel, it is difficult to take the fixtures seriously. Nevertheless, here follows a record of Arsenal and Chelsea contests during the Great War, which produced a number of 'freak results.

CHELSEA 3   ARSENAL 1   October 30th 1915 (Crowd: 12,500)

Goalscorers: Croal(2) Thomson   Moore

CHELSEA	ARSENAL
1 Hampton	1 Kempton
2 Marshall	2 Sands
3 Harrow	3 Shaw
4 Taylor	4 Ducat
5 Middleboe	5 Buckley
6 Halse	6 Bradshaw

7 Ford	7 Wallace
8 Buchan	8 Groves
9 Thomson	9 King
10 Croal	10 Moore
11 Moores	11 Lewis
ARSENAL 0	CHELSEA 6

6 January 15th 1916 (Crowd: 15000)

Goalscorers: Ford (3) Buchan(2)   Thomson

ARSENAL	CHELSEA
1 Kempton	1 Hampton
2 Sands	2 Marshall
3 Shaw	3 Harrow
4 Ducat	4 Taylor
5 Buckley	5 Bettridge
6 Grant	6 Halse
7 Wallace	7 Ford
8 Thompson	8 Buchan
9 King	9 Thomson
10 Bradshaw	10 Steer
11 Rutherford	11 Croal

LONDON COMBINATION:

CHELSEA 1st Won 17 Drew3 Lost 2 Goals for 71 Against 18 Points 37
ARSENAL 3rd Won 10 Drew 5 Lost 7 Goals for 43 Against 46 Points 25
   CHELSEA 9   ARSENAL   0   April   21st   1916
(Crowd: 26,000) Goalscorers: Buchan(4) Thomson (5)

Charlie Buchan and Bob Thomson were the goalscoring heroes whose demolition of the Gunners remains the "unofficial" highest score involvingArsenal and Chelsea. Buchan finished the season with forty goals from only thirty appearances, while Thomson recorded thirty eight goals from just /thirty one outings. Both these deadly marksmen were instrumental in ensuring that the west Londoners would win both the first competition and the subsidiary competition of the London Combination.

CHELSEA	ARSENAL
1 Whitley	1 Kempton
2 Spratt	2 Bradshaw
3 Harrow	3 Bourne
4 Taylor	4 Morris
5 Middleboe	5 Liddell
6 Halse	6 McKinnon
7 Ford	7 Lewis
8 Buchan	8 Broderick
9 Thomson	9 Chipperfield
10 Croal	10 Lees
11 Bridgeman	11 Elkington

ARSENAL 1   CHELSEA 3

April 24th 1916 (Crowd : 13000)

Goalscorers: Groves Buchan Thomson(2)

ARSENAL	CHELSEA
1 Cooper	1 Whitley
2 Sands	2 Marshall
3 Shaw	3 Harrow

4 Ducat	4 Taylor
5 Buckley	5 Bettridge
6 Bradshaw	6 Halse
7 Rutherford	7 Nicholls
8 Groves	8 Buchan
9 Chipperfield	9 Thomson
10 Lees	10 Croal
11 Elkington	11 Bridgeman

1916 SUBSIDIARY COMPETITION:

CHELSEA 1st Won 10 Drew1 Lost 3 Goals for 50 Against 15 Points 21
ARSENAL 11th Won 3 Drew 4 Lost 7 Goals for 19 Against 31 Points 10

CHELSEA 3   ARSENAL 0 September30th
1916 (Crowd 12,000)

Goalscorers: Thomson Middleboe Freeman

CHELSEA	ARSENAL
1 Denoon	1 Williamson
2 D. Taylor	2 Bradshaw
3 Harrow	3 Hutchins
4 F.Taylor	4 Allman
5 Middleboe	5 Stapley
6 Halse	6 Knowles
7 Ford	7 Rutherford
8 Freeman	8 Williams
9 Thomson	9 King
10 Croal	10 Hardinge
11 Bridgeman	11 Elkington

ARSENAL 2   CHELSEA 1
December 23rd 1916 (Crowd: 8000)

Goalscorers; Hardinge Chipperfield Spratt

ARSENAL	CHELSEA
1 Williamson	1 Hughes
2 Bradshaw	2 Worrall
3 Hutchins	3 Harrow
4 Allman	4 Spratt
5 Liddell	5 Davidson
6 McKinnon	6 Middleboe
7 Rutherford	7 Bresname
8 F.Groves	8 Halse
9 Hardinge	9 Thomson
10 Chipperfield	10 D.Taylor
11 Elkington	11 Kelly

ARSENAL 3   CHELSEA 0
February 17th 1917 (Crowd 7,500)

Goalscorers: Hardinge F Groves Rutherford

ARSENAL	CHELSEA
1 Williamson	1 Hughes
2 Bradshaw	2 D.Taylor
3 Hutchins	3 Harrow
4 Grant	4 Middleboe
5 Buckley	5 Spratt
6 Chipperfield	6 Jackson
7 Rutherford	7 Campbell
8 F.Groves	8 Newman
9 Spittle	9 Thomson

10Hardinge   10 Croal
11 Wilkins   11 Kelly

CHELSEA 2   ARSENAL 0
March 31st 1917 (Crowd 6,000)

Goalscorers: Croal Halse

CHELSEA	ARSENAL
1 Hughes	1 Williamson
2 Worrall	2 Bradshaw
3 D. Taylor	3 Hutchins
4 Spratt	4 Chipperfield
5 Middleboe	5 Stapley
6 A.N.Other	6 McKinnon
7 Campbell	7 F.Groves
8 Halse	8 H.Groves
9 Thomson	9 Hardinge
10 Croal	10 Spittle
11 Kelly	11 Wilkins

LONDON COMBINATION 1916-1917 ARSENAL 2nd
(Full statistics unavailable)
CHELSEA 3rd (Full statistics unavailable)

ARSENAL 0   CHELSEA 1
September 29th 1917 (Crowd 16.000)

Goalscorer: Halse

ARSENAL   CHELSEA

1 Williamson	1 Hughes
2 Bradshaw	2 Hendon
3 Hutchins	3 Taylor
4 Grant	4 Cadman
5 Liddell	5 Dickie
6 McKinnon	6 Middleboe
7 Rutherford	7 Bresname
8 F.Groves	8 Halse
9 Pagnam	9 Thomson
10 Chipperfield	10 Freeman
11 Lewis	11 Croal

CHELSEA 4   ARSENAL 3
November 24th 1917 (Crowd 6,000)
Goalscorers: Croal Thomson(2) Taylor;
Bradshaw(pen)Rutherford Groves

CHELSEA	ARSENAL
1 Hughes	1 Williamson
2 Middleboe	2 Bradshaw
3 Taylor	3 Cockerill
4 Barber	4 Grant
5 Nicholson	5 Stapley
6 Kimberley	6 Chipperfield
7 Rolls	7 Rutherford
8 Bridgeman	8 F.Groves
9 Thomson	9 Pagnam
10 Croal	10 Blyth
11 Kelly	11 Ison

ARSENAL 4　　　　CHELSEA 1
January 19th 1918 (Crowd 7,000)
Goalscorers: Hardinge Rutherford
Groves Lewis; Abrams

ARSENAL	CHELSEA
1 Williamson	1 Molyneux
2 Bradshaw	2 Barber
3 Hutchins	3 Taylor
4 Ducat	4 Compton
5 Liddell	5 Nicholls
6 Cockerill	6 White
7 Rutherford	7 Kelly
8 F.Groves	8 Abrams
9 Hardinge	9 Smith
10 Baker	10 Freeman
11 Lewis	11 Croal

CHELSEA 4   ARSENAL 2
March 16th 1918 (Crowd 4,000)
Goalscorers: Halse Smith(2) Langford;
Chipperfield Douglas

CHELSEA   ARSENAL
1 Hughes   1 Williamson
2 Middleboe   2 Bradshaw
3 Taylor   3 Hutchins
4 Compton   4 Ducat
5 Jackson   5 Liddell
6 Nicholson   6 Stapley
7 Charles   7 Rutherford
8 Langford   8 F.Groves
9 Halse   9 Douglas
10 Smith   10 Chipperfield
11 Casey   11 Lewis

LONDON COMBINATION: 1917-18

CHELSEA 1st Won 21 Drew8 Lost 7   Goals for 82 Against
39 Points 50
ARSENAL 5th Won 16 Drew 5 Lost 15 Goals for 76 Against
57 Points 37

CHELSEA 4   ARSENAL 1
October19th 1918 (Crowd 25,000)
Goalscorers: Kelly (3) Rolyat; Spittle

CHELSEA   ARSENAL
1 Hughes   1 Williamson
2 Middleboe   2 Shaw

3 Taylor	3 Hutchins
4 Godson	4 Ducat
5 Smith	5 Gregory
6 Pacey	6 Liddell
7 Rolyat	7 Groves
8 Langford	8 Spittle
9 Casey	9 Hardinge
10 Kelly	10 Bradshaw
11 Adams	11 Chipperfield

ARSENAL 3   CHELSEA 0

December 14th 1918 (Crowd 8,000)

Goalscorers: Chipperfield Dominy Thompson

ARSENAL	CHELSEA
1 Williamson	1 Hughes
2 Shaw	2 Bettridge
3 Hutchins	3 Harrow
4 Ducat	4 Middleboe
5 Liddell	5 Davidson
6 Williams	6 Pacey
7 Groves	7 Bird
8 Dominy	8 Fazackerley
9 Thompson	9 Taylor
10 Bradshaw	10 Freeman
11 Chipperfield	11 Casey

CHELSEA 1   ARSENAL 2

February 8th 1919 (Crowd 16,000)

Goalscorers: Ford; Hardinge Chipperfield

CHELSEA	ARSENAL
1 Hughes	1 Williamson
2 Bettridge	2 Bradshaw
3 Harrow	3 Shaw
4 Davidson	4 Ducat
5 Middleboe	5 Liddell
6 Halse	6 McKinnon
7 Ford	7 Groves
8 Jack	8 Robson
9 Brittan	9 Miller
10 Freeman	10 Hardinge
11 Bridgeman	11 Chipperfield

ARSENAL 2   CHELSEA 1
April 5th 1919 (Crowd 35,000)

Goalscorers: Hardinge Rutherford; Wilding

ARSENAL	CHELSEA
1 Williamson	1 Molyneux
2 Liddell	2 Bettridge
3 Hutchins	3 Harrow
4 Jobey	4 Casey
5 Plumb	5 Wright
6 McKinnon	6 Ramsay
7 Rutherford	7 Ford
8 Robson	8 Whittingham
9 Hardinge	9 Wilding
10 Spittle	10 Freeman
11 Chipperfield	11 Croal

WARTIME DERBY ENCOUNTERS (1939-1946)

After the bitter experiences of the Great War, the English Football League was under no illusions about a quick solution when Neville Chamberlain's National Government declared war on Nazi Germany on the first weekend of September 1939. Consequently, unlike in 1914, the Division One programme was suspended immediately (with each club having competed in three league outings).

Once again, English football was re-organised on a regional basis for the duration of the new world conflict. Arsenal and Chelsea continued their local skirmishes to provide a boost to the morale on the Home Front, but with many players contributing to the war effort, it is difficult to take the following results too seriously.

Nevertheless, with Arsenal and Chelsea playing their part in providing a distraction from the anxieties of war, the encounters between the two clubs have been listed here – for the record.

ARSENAL 3   CHELSEA 0 March 23rd 1940 (Crowd 15,000) Goalscorers: D.Compton L. Compton Weaver(OG)

ARSENAL	CHELSEA
1 Swindin	1 Jackson
2 Male	2 O'Hare
3 Hapgood	3 Barber
4 Crayston	4 Mayes
5 Joy	5 Salmond
6 L.Jones	6 Weaver

7 Kirchen	7 Spence
8 Lewis	8 Kiernan
9 L.Compton	9 Payne
10 B.Jones	10 Smith
11 D.Compton	11 Alexander

CHELSEA 2   ARSENAL 2
April 17th 1940 (Crowd 8,500)

Goalscorers: Weaver Payne; Lewis(2)

CHELSEA	ARSENAL
1 Jackson	1 Wilson
2 O'Hare	2 Male
3 Reay	3 Hapgood
4 Lowe	4 Crayston
5 Ridyard	5 Joy
6 Weaver	6 L.Jones
7 Buchanan	7 Drake
8 Kiernan	8 Lewis
9 Payne	9 L.Compton
10 Foss	10 Curtis
11 Alexander	11 Bastin

FOOTBALL LEAGUE SOUTH GROUP C

ARSENAL 3rd Won 9 Drew 5 Lost 4   Goals for 41 Against 26 Points 23
CHESEA 9th Won 4 Drew 3 Lost 11 Goals for 33 Against 53 Points 11

CHELSEA 3   ARSENAL 1 April 14th 1941
(Crowd 4.000)

Goalscorers: Mills J.Smith G.Smith; Nelson

CHELSEA	ARSENAL
1 Woodley	1 Boulton
2 Barber	2 Scott
3 Griffiths	3 Hapgood
4 Tennant	4 Henley
5 G.Smith	5 L.Compton
6 Weaver	6 Collett
7 Spence	7 Kirchen
8 J.Smith	8 Lewis
9 Mills	9 Drake
10 A.N.Other	10 Nelson
11 Foss	11 Bastin

ARSENAL 3   CHELSEA 0
October 4th 1941 (Crowd 7,747)

Goalscorers: Lewis Crayston Weaver(OG))

ARSENAL	CHELSEA
1 Platt	1 Woodley
2 Scott	2 Hardwick
3 L.Compton	3 Johnson
4 Crayston	4 Tennant
5 Joy	5 Salmond
6 Collett	6 Weaver
7 Drake	7 C.Smith
8 Kirchen	8 Kiernan
9 Lewis	9 Clements
10 Nelson	10 Galloway
11 Bastin	11 Spence

CHELSEA 1   ARSENAL 5
January 10th 1942 (Crowd 12,260)

Goalscorers: Weale; L.Compton(2) Miller

Kirchen(2)

Leslie Compton, who scored twice here, made a guest appearance for Chelsea eight weeks later.

CHELSEA	ARSENAL
1 Jackson	1 Marks
2 Craig	2 Male
3 Hardwick	3 Hapgood
4 Tennant	4 Crayston
5 Griffiths	5 Joy
6 Weaver	6 Collett
7 Spence	7 Kirchen
8 Galloway	8 Miller
9 Kurz	9 L.Compton
10 Peacock	10 Henley
11 Weale	11 Bastin

LONDON WAR LEAGUE 1941-1942

ARSENAL 1st Won 23 Drew 2 Lost 5   Goals for 108 Against 43 Points 48

CHESEA 13th Won 8 Drew 4 Lost 18 Goals for 56 Against 88 Points 20

CHELSEA 5   ARSENAL 2 December 25th 1942 (Crowd 17,000)

Goalscorers: Bryant(4) Liddell; Lewis Colley

Arsenal and Chelsea. like all other clubs, accommodated various guest players who made occasional appearances when there were vacancies in a team. In this Christmas day encounter, future England manager Walter Winterbottom helped to contribute to the home team's crushing victory. Matt Busby, Ron Greenwood and Joe Mercer were three other future managers who made guest appearances for Chelsea during the Second World War.

CHELSEA	ARSENAL
1 Woodley	1 Watson-Smith
2 Winterbottom	2 Scott
3 Farmer	3 Hapgood
4 Bidewell	4 Pryde
5 Allen	5 Male
6 Bearryman	6 Bastin
7 Spence	7 Colley
8 Mckennan	8 Drake
9 Bryant	9 Lewis
10 Foss	10 Nelson
11 Liddell	11 Cumner

ARSENAL 1   CHELSEA 5
December 26th 1942 (Crowd18,253)

Goalscorers: Bastin; Mckennan(3) Spence(2)

After bulging Arsenal's net five times on the previous day, Billy Birrell's team were not surprisingly unchanged for the Boxing Day fixture. Another five goal haul was achieved which represented Chelsea's first "major" win at Highbury since September 1917. Although the Blues recorded two narrow wins in friendly games at Arsenal in 1915 and 1925, this triumph ended a miserable sequence of thirteen defeats in league and FA Cup matches when the Pensioners visited Highbury.

ARSENAL	CHELSEA
1 Watson-Smith	1 Woodley

2 Scott	2 Winterbottom
3 Young	3 Farmer
4 Pryde	4 Bidewell
5 Male	5 Allen
6 Hapgood	6 Bearryman
7 Colley	7 Spence
8 Drake	8 Mckennan
9 Lewis	9 Bryant
10 Bastin	10 Foss
11 Cumner	11 Liddell

FOOTBALL LEAGUE SOUTH 1942-1943

ARSENAL 1st Won 21 Drew 1 Lost 6   Goals for 102 Against 35 Points 43
CHELSEA 7th Won 14 Drew 4 Lost 10 Goals for 52 Against 45 Points 32

ARSENAL 6   CHELSEA 0
November 6th 1943 (Crowd16,007)
Goalscorers: Lewis(2) Bastin(2) D.Compton(2)
This emphatic result stands as Arsenal's "unofficial" highest win against Chelsea.

ARSENAL	CHELSEA
1 Swindin	1 Jackson
2 Male	2 Dyer
3 Barnes	3 Westwood
4 Crayston	4 Russell
5 Joy	5 Harris
6 Collett	6 Foss

7 Briscoe	7 Spence
8 Curtis	8 Hinchliffe
9 Lewis	9 Payne
10 Bastin	10 Stewart
11 D.Compton	11 Mitten

CHELSEA 2   ARSENAL 0
January 8th 1944 (Crowd : 19,310)
Goalscorer:: Payne(2)

A double from the prolific Joe Payne avenged the 6-0 defeat by the visitors two months earlier.It took place in front of Stamford Bridge1s largest crowd since the eve of war in August 1939.

CHELSEA	ARSENAL
1 Woodley	1 Marks
2 Hardwick	2 Male
3 Westwood	3 Scott
4 Russell	4 Collett
5 Harris	5 Joy
6 Martin	6 Edlington
7 Ashcroft	7 Briscoe
8 Tennant	8 Drake
9 Payne	9 Lewis
10 Foss	10 Bastin
11 Mitten	11 D.Compton

FOOTBALL LEAGUE SOUTH 1943-1944

ARSENAL 4th Won 14 Drew 10 Lost 6 Goals for 72 Against 42 Points 38

CHELSEA 8th Won 16 Drew 2 Lost 12 Goals for 79
Against 55 Points 34
> CHELSEA 2 ARSENAL 1:
> November 25th 1944 (Crowd 37,753)
> Goalscorers: Payne Machin; Steele

CHELSEA	ARSENAL
1 Anderson	1 Swindin
2 Winter	2 Male
3 Hapgood	3 Mennie
4 Russell	4 Bastin
5 Harris	5 Tunnicliffe
6 Foss	6 Collett
7 Wardle	7 Farquhar
8 Hurrell	8 Smith
9 Payne	9 Steele
10 Machin	10 Morrad
11 Mitten	11 Wrigglesworth

> ARSENAL 3 CHELSEA 0;
> April 28th 1945 (Crowd10,349)
> Goalscorers: Drake Farquhar Bastin

Ten days before the successful conclusion of the Second World War (in Europe), the Gunners themselves were taking care of some unfinished business. Having lost twice to the Pensioners in 1944, the home team proceeded to obtain vengeance with a convincing win. This occasion was notable as being the last time the deadly duo Cliff Bastin and Ted Drake would terrorise any Chelsea goalkeeper with goals. Drake's next involvement in this London derby would be in the capacity of Chelsea manager in 1953

ARSENAL	CHELSEA
1 Marks	1 Black
2 Scott	2 Cowan
3 Barnes	3 Dawes
4 Henley	4 Russell
5 Hall	5 Franks
6 Hamilton	6 Foss
7 Farquhar	7 Wardle
8 Harris	8 Tennant
9 Drake	9 Bidewell
10 Bastin	10 Hurrell
11 Taylor	11 McDonald

FOOTBALL LEAGUE SOUTH 1944-1945

CHELSEA 4th Won 16 Drew 5 Lost 9   Goals for 100
Against 55 Points 37
ARSENAL 8th Won 14 Drew 3 Lost 13 Goals for 77
Against 67 Points 31
ARSENAL 1   CHELSEA 2;
March 9th 1946 (Crowd30,554)
Goalscorers: D.Compton; Lawton Spence

Tommy Lawton, probably England's finest centre forward
at this time, scored in his first appearance inthis particular
derby. Lawton, along with George Graham in the 1960's
would not only go on to represent both clubs ,but would
also score for both Arsenal and Chelsea when they
confronted one another.

ARSENAL	CHELSEA
1 Swindin	1 Robertson
2 Male	2 Winter

3 Scott   3 Tennant
4 Waller   4 Armstrong
5 Joy   5 Harris
6 Patterson   6 Foss
7 Nelson   7 Spence
8 Jones   8 Brindle
9 O'Flanagan   9 Lawton
10 Bastin   10 Williams
11 D.Compton   11 Dolding

CHELSEA 1   **ARSENAL 2**
March 16th 1946 (Crowd 45,000)
Goalscorers: Brindle; D.Compton (2)

Although hostilities had ceased in the Far East in August 1945, the Football League South was expected to run its course during this transitional year. In their last "war-time" engagement against each other, Denis Compton's pair of goals avenged the previous week's defeat by the same score when the England and Middlesex cricketing legend also scored.

CHELSEA   ARSENAL
1 Robertson   1 Swindin
2 White   2 Scott
3 Tennant   3 Collett
4 Armstrong   4 Nelson
5 Harris   5 Joy
6 Foss   6 Waller
7 Spence   7 O'Flanagan
8 Brindle   8 McPherson
9 Lawton   9 Barnard
10 Williams   10 Bastin

11 Dolding   11 D.Compton

FOOTBALL LEAGUE SOUTH 1945-1946

CHELSEA 10th Won 19 Drew 6 Lost 17   Goals for 92
Against 80 Points 44
ARSENAL 11th Won 16 Drew 11 Lost 15 Goals for 76
Against 73 Points 43

'OTHER GAMES'

In cricketing parlance, the following exchanges between
Arsenal and Chelsea may not be first-class fixtures, but
nevertheless the assortment below still deserve to be
recorded.

Dec. 7th 1908   Chelsea 0   Woolwich Arsenal 1 (London
PFA Charity Fund)
Sept. 4th 1911   Chelsea 0   Woolwich Arsenal 2 (London
PFA Charity Fund)
Oct 16th 1911   Woolwich Arsenal 2 Chelsea 3 (London
FA Challenge Cup round 2)
Oct 30th 1911   Woolwich Arsenal 1 Chelsea 0 (London
FA Challenge Cup round 2) replay
Sept 30th 1912   Chelsea 1   Woolwich Arsenal 3 (London
PFA Charity Fund)
Oct 20th 1913 Chelsea 0   Woolwich Arsenal 1 London
FA Challenge Cup round 2)
May 17th 1919 Arsenal 1   Chelsea 2   (Friendly)
Oct 27th 1924   Arsenal 2   Chelsea 0   London FA
Challenge Cup round 1)
Jan 31st 1925 Arsenal 0   Chelsea 1   (Friendly)

Nov 13th 1933   Arsenal 3   Chelsea 2   London FA
Challenge Cup Semi-Final)
Oct 7th   1939   Chelsea 0   Arsenal 3   (Friendly)

The above match was arranged hastily after the outbreak of
war had suspended the normal football league programme
indefinitely.
Oct 25th   1948   Chelsea 4   Arsenal 1 (London FA
Challenge Cup round 2)
Dec 7th   1953   Chelsea 1   Arsenal 1 (London FA
Challenge Cup Final)
March 29th 1954   Arsenal 3   Chelsea 2 (London FA
Challenge Cup Replay)
Nov 1st   1954   Arsenal 4   Chelsea 1 (London FA
Challenge Cup Semi-Final)
Oct 15th   1959   Arsenal 1   Chelsea 2 (London FA
Challenge Cup round 2)
Dec 5th   1960   Chelsea 3   Arsenal 1 (London FA
Challenge Cup Final)
Dec 3rd   1962   Arsenal 4   Chelsea 1 (London FA
Challenge Cup Final)
Oct 21st   1963   Chelsea 3   Arsenal 0 (London FA
Challenge Cup round 2)
Nov 6th   1974   Chelsea 1   Arsenal 1 (John Hollins
Testimonial)
March 26th 1977 Chelsea 3   Arsenal 0   (Friendly)
Aug 20th   1982   Chelsea 1   Arsenal 3   (Friendly)
Nov 1st   1983   Chelsea 2   Arsenal 1 (Mickey Droy
Testimonial)

Tony Adams made his first team debut in the above
encounter.